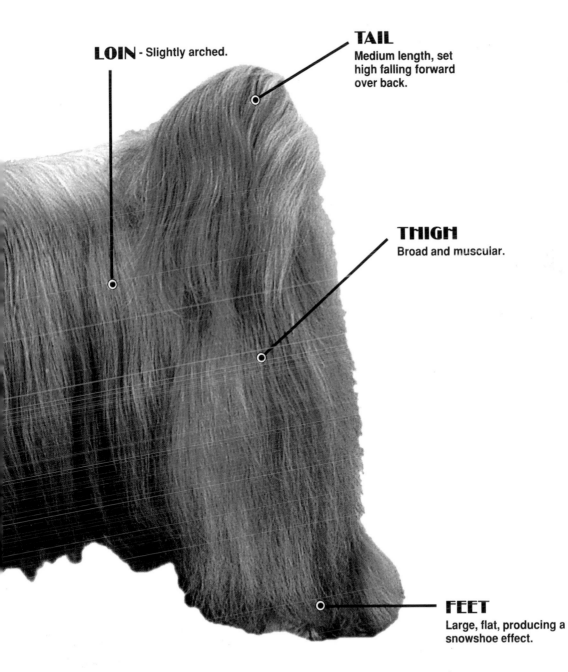

LOIN - Slightly arched.

TAIL
Medium length, set
high falling forward
over back.

THIGH
Broad and muscular.

FEET
Large, flat, producing a
snowshoe effect.

Title page: Tibetan Terrier photographed by Isabelle Francais.

Photographers: Mary Bloom, Paulette Braun, Bonnie Brock, Dorothy Chase, Toodie Connor, DVM, Dean Dennis, Beverly and Ken Edmonds, Isabelle Francais, Judy Iby.

© by T.F.H. Publications, Inc.

Distributed in the UNITED STATES to the Pet Trade by T.F.H. Publications, Inc., One T.F.H. Plaza, Neptune City, NJ 07753; distributed in the UNITED STATES to the Bookstore and Library Trade by National Book Network, Inc. 4720 Boston Way, Lanham MD 20706; in CANADA to the Pet Trade by H & L Pet Supplies Inc., 27 Kingston Crescent, Kitchener, Ontario N2B 2T6; Rolf C. Hagen Inc., 3225 Sartelon St. Laurent-Montreal Quebec H4R 1E8; in CANADA to the Book Trade by Vanwell Publishing Ltd., 1 Northrup Crescent, St. Catharines, Ontario L2M 6P5 ; in ENGLAND by T.F.H. Publications, PO Box 15, Waterlooville PO7 6BQ; in AUSTRALIA AND THE SOUTH PACIFIC by T.F.H. (Australia), Pty. Ltd., Box 149, Brookvale 2100 N.S.W., Australia; in NEW ZEALAND by Brooklands Aquarium Ltd. 5 McGiven Drive, New Plymouth, RD1 New Zealand; in Japan by T.F.H. Publications, Japan—Jiro Tsuda, 10-12-3 Ohjidai, Sakura, Chiba 285, Japan; in SOUTH AFRICA by Lopis (Pty) Ltd., P.O. Box 39127, Booysens, 2016, Johannesburg, South Africa. Published by T.F.H. Publications, Inc.

MANUFACTURED IN THE
UNITED STATES OF AMERICA
BY T.F.H. PUBLICATIONS, INC.

TIBETAN TERRIER

A COMPLETE AND RELIABLE HANDBOOK

Anne Keleman

RX-132

CONTENTS

DESCRIPTION OF THE TIBETAN TERRIER

The Tibetan Terrier evolved over many centuries, surviving in Tibet's extreme climate and difficult terrain. The breed developed a protective double coat, compact size, unique foot structure and great agility.

He is a medium-sized dog and falls into 50-50 proportions. That is, his body is as long as he is tall; his skull is half muzzle and half head, measuring from the tip of the nose to the corner of the eye and from the corner of the eye to the top of the head. (*Author's note:* Although visually the head looks to be of 50-50 proportions, in an exchange of measurements with an English breeder a few years ago, it was found that the muzzle is five to ten percent shorter than the measurement of the corner of the eye to the occiput. This is a matter of interpretation and offered as an unofficial observation.) When looked at straight-on, his eyes are in the center of his head, much as a human's eyes are in the center of the head.

The Tibetan Terrier has evolved over many centuries, surviving harsh climates and difficult terrain. Ch. Rje-Bo's Decatur's Clairmont owned by Beverly and Ken Edmonds.

DESCRIPTION

He is profusely coated, powerfully built, with a well-feathered tail that curls up and falls over his back. A fall of hair covers his eyes and foreface. When viewed from the side, he is a well proportioned, compact, square dog. His lower jaw has a small beard and his nose should be black. The mouth has three acceptable closures, with the scissors bite preferred by most people; a tight reverse scissors bite (undershot) and a level bite are equally acceptable in the standard. The reverse scissors bite must never be faulted, as it plays an important part in avoiding snipeyness. The teeth should fall into a distinct curve between the canines. The eyes should be dark, set wide apart, and the eye rims should also be dark.

His neck is proportionate to the body and the head. The chest and legs should be heavily furnished. His shoulders should be sloping, well muscled and well laid back. The legs are straight and strong when viewed from the front. The feet make the Tibetan Terrier unique. They are large, flat and round, producing a snowshoe effect. In some sections of the US where a weed commonly called the "foxtail" is prevalent, it may be necessary to remove the hair between the toes and the bottom of the pads, as this weed, shaped like an airplane, will penetrate the flesh and

The Tibetan Terrier's dark eyes are found in the center of his head, much like a person, and are framed by his characteristic eyelashes. Owner, Bonnie Brock.

requires the services of a veterinarian for removal. For show purposes, the standard demands that the foot be trimmed level, if at all.

The hind legs are heavily furnished and slightly longer than the forelegs. Hocks are low-set and turn neither in nor out. Dewclaws may be removed. The Tibetan Terrier has a free, effortless stride with good reach in front and flexibility in the rear allowing full extension. When gaiting, the hind legs should go neither inside nor outside the front legs but should move on the same track, approaching single tracking when the dog is moving at a fast trot. He is also a dog of remarkable speed and could possibly rank with the fastest of dogs.

The coat is described as double with the undercoat soft and woolly; the outer coat is either wavy or straight, never curly. The coat should not hang to the ground; an area of light should be seen under the dog. Sculpturing, scissoring, stripping and shaving are contrary to the breed and are serious faults, although one sees more and more of this in the show ring. For ease of care and for household pets, the coat is of

The profuse double coat of the Tibetan should have a soft, woolly texture and hang straight and flat without curling. Ch. Da-Rista Joshua of Clairmont owned by Beverly and Ken Edmonds.

DESCRIPTION

such texture that a professional groomer is able to put him in any kind of pattern. The coat color is also unique in the world of dogs. Every color or color combination is represented. There are no preferred colors or color combinations.

The size of the Tibetan Terrier ranges from 20 to 24 pounds, but may be 18 to 30 pounds. The proportion of weight to height is more important than the specific

The breed standard is the basis upon which dogs are judges for conformation shows. "Zorro," with his owner Louise Acker, takes Group One.

weight. It should reflect a well-balanced, square dog. The height of the dog is 15 to 16 inches, with bitches slightly smaller; the ideal is 14 to 16 inches at the shoulder. Any height above 17 inches or below 14 inches is a serious fault.

The Tibetan Terrier is highly intelligent, sensitive, loyal, devoted and affectionate. The breed may be cautious or reserved. Extreme shyness is a fault.

Present-day standards in all countries today reflect Dr. Greig's opinions, and where she appeared insistent, it was her strong desire to lean toward perfection. On the other hand, where questions were raised, for instance, regarding mouth closures or measurements on which the Tibetan Terrier should be judged, it was mainly due to a choice of words the British used as compared to American descriptions: i.e., "pincer bite"

The coat of Tibetan Terrier puppies is shorter and often has a softer texture than that of adults. Owner, Toodie Connor, DVM.

and/or "withers" and "point of shoulder." There was also a typographical error made early in the history of the Tibetan Terrier when the size was printed as 14 to 16 inches at the shoulder. It was meant to state 14 to 17 inches at the shoulder. By the time Dr. Greig discovered this, the standard had been printed and the size remained as printed. However, time proved Dr. Greig correct in the matter of size, and she always claimed that the overall balance was of prime consideration. Today more and more standardization of size is evident.

ORIGIN OF THE TIBETAN TERRIER

The origin of the Tibetan Terrier is shrouded in mystery. Although the breed is said to have existed for over 2000 years, record keeping only began in the 1930s. It is believed that the Tibetan Terrier originally came from the region that is called "The Lost Valley of Tibet." Heads of monasteries visiting the valley prior

Where did we come from? The origin of the Tibetan Terrier is shrouded in mystery. Puppies owned by Toodie Connor, DVM.

to the great earthquake, which took place over 600 years ago and which destroyed the road leading to the valley, were given a Tibetan Terrier upon their departure to bring "peace and prosperity" to their respective monasteries. Eventually the name "peace-bringer" became "luck-bringer." Later they were awarded as gifts to those who performed a great service or earned the gratitude of a Tibetan Terrier owner.

Tibetan Terriers became so highly prized that the dogs were hidden from strangers and the owners denied all knowledge of their existence. After the early monastery dogs, they began to appear in Tibetan households, where they were equally cherished and treated as children—the name given to them was "little people." As they became more readily available, they soon joined the nomads and became a part of the caravans. Because it was believed that they brought good luck, and because they performed numerous duties, the dogs became very useful in the harsh existence of the nomadic tribes.

TIBETANS GO WEST

The Tibetan Terrier was introduced into the western world by Dr. Agnes R.H. Greig, a British surgeon stationed in India. Dr. Greig had performed major surgery on the wife of a Tibetan tribesman and in gratitude they rewarded her with a female Tibetan Terrier puppy. Dr. Greig was enchanted with her new acquisition. She was already showing dogs and horses in India, so she contacted the secretary of the Indian Kennel Club, Mr. Medley, who was also a well-known judge of dogs. He suggested that she register her little dog as a Lhasa Terrier so that it could be shown. When the judges saw the dog, they all agreed that it was not a Lhasa Terrier (as Lhasa Apsos were known at that time) and that they had never seen a dog of this type. It was suggested to her that she obtain a mate for her dog and breed a litter to see if the dogs bred

The Tibetan Terrier was highly prized in his native land of Tibet and was often given to people as a token of luck or gratitude. Ch. Bel Fluer of Tamridge owned by Bonnie Brock.

true. Dr. Greig contacted her friends and they brought her a male. She was told to keep the whole litter from the resultant mating and show the pups to Mr. Medley when they were three months old, at which time he would select a puppy to be bred back to a parent.

Dr. Greig later took all three generations to the Delhi show where a panel of judges were to decide if indeed they were purebreds. The panel of judges examined the three generations and pronounced them purebreds. They also decided to name them "Tibetan Terriers," probably because they were of the popular terrier size. Dr. Greig then had to re-apply to the Indian Kennel Club to transfer her dogs from Lhasa Terriers to Tibetan Terriers.

While the dogs were in the process of being transferred from one breed to the other in India, Dr. Greig had been given a leave and was off to England with her dogs. Since she wanted to show them in England, they had to be registered as Lhasa Terriers, as the transfer had not yet been made in India. At that time, India was a British colony. Dr. Greig then had to ask the Indian Kennel Club to transfer the dogs to the corrected name with the English Kennel Club. The transfer was eventually made and they were officially known in Britain as "Tibetan Terriers."

The doctor served in India for 12 years, and during that period she took several more Tibetan Terriers to England to establish her Lamleh line. Her sister and mother had other breeds but also bred Tibetan Terriers to a lesser degree, under the prefix "Ladlok." Along with her Tibetan Terriers, Dr. Greig had also imported Tibetan Spaniels and Lhasa Terriers, and these breeds were also under the Lamleh and Ladlok prefixes.

During the war years, Dr. Greig, her mother and her sister were desperately trying to save their canine companions and even resorted to raising rabbits to help feed their dogs. Her Lhasa Apsos and Tibetan Spaniels succumbed because of the lack of vaccines, but the Tibetan Terriers survived the ravages of hard-pad disease, today known as distemper.

Before the war years, the doctor had been shipping her best dogs back to India and to various European countries. There was one established Tibetan Terrier breeder in Germany, but all of her dogs were shot during the war so unfortunately those lines were lost.

After the war, Dr. Greig was breeding again, and while she distrusted her English countrymen, she was again shipping her dogs back to India and France, Germany, Italy, and Switzerland. Since she had almost total control over the breed, for many years it was impossible to obtain one of these dogs in England. Single-handedly she was breeding and registering her dogs to meet the requirements of the Kennel Club.

It is commonly thought that the Lamleh line consisted only of the original dogs brought back from India by Dr. Greig. (In those days women were not allowed to enter Tibet; therefore, all of her transactions to obtain dogs from Tibet were made in India.)

Thanks to the breeding program of Dr. Agnes Greig and subsequent breeding programs, the Tibetan Terrier was saved from extinction.

This is not the case, as she diluted the pedigrees of her dogs with a few other dogs brought back by service people from Tibet. From these breedings, most of the Tibetan Terriers in the world descend.

After the war years, a small dog was found wandering on the docks of Liverpool where it was assumed he had jumped a ship from India. He was taken to the kennels of John and Constance Downey, who were well known in the dog world. At the insistence of several of their friends prominent in judging dogs, the dog was presented to a panel of judges and certified as a Tibetan Terrier. He was named Trojan Kynos. The Downeys had obtained a gold female named Princess Aureus, whose dam was of unknown origin but had been bred to one of Dr. Greig's dogs. Princess

Aureus was bred to Trojan Kynos and thus the Luneville line was established. As the Luneville dogs began to win in the show ring, a bitter rivalry developed with Dr. Greig's complaints that the Luneville dogs were not purebreds. The complaints became so numerous that the Kennel Club finally decreed that Dr. Greig refrain from further accusations regarding the Luneville dogs.

Later, an attempt at a reconciliation resulted in a mating between Downey's bitch (a daughter of the bitterly criticized Ch. Trojan Kynos) and one of Dr. Greig's best dogs, Ch. Kala Kah of Lamleh. The doctor had willingly consented to this breeding in a charitable moment. The reconciliation was short-lived and one wonders why she permitted the breeding, which firmly established the Luneville line. The feud continued.

Despite controversy between early Tibetan Terrier breeders, the breed flourished in England and continues to gain popularity today.

Dr. Greig found unexpected support for her Lamleh line in 1956. Dr. and Mrs. Harry Murphy of Great Falls, Virginia, were looking for a shaggy dog for their daughter. They purchased through an agent, and so the first official Tibetan Terrier was imported into the United States. She came from Dr. Greig's kennels. There had been other Tibetan Terriers brought into the US that were simply pets, one of which belonged to a famous opera star who had come to Hollywood to make musicals. The Murphys became enchanted (as was Dr. Greig with her first dog) and contacted her for a male. Thus the Lamleh of Kalai line was established in the United States in 1957.

Dr. and Mrs. Murphy became good friends of Dr. Greig, who was still reluctant to place her dogs in Britain and continued to send her best dogs to the

Murphys in the United States. Copies of transfer papers show that some of these dogs were shipped to the Murphy's daughter, Patricia, as the consignee.

In the United States, Mrs. Murphy followed in the footsteps of Dr. Greig in England, displaying the same protective pattern in placing her dogs only with people she trusted, and for many years these little dogs were available only to those closely associated with her.

Soon dogs were arriving from England (some from Dr. Greig) and a further integration of the two lines gained a foothold. Meanwhile, in England, partisans began taking sides, but the well-groomed Luneville dogs in the show ring began to overtake the presence of the Lamleh dogs. One would have assumed that the sharp division of opinion between the two lines originating in England would have been resolved by this time. However, it continued into the United States. The bitter feud is part of the history of the Tibetan Terrier and we owe it to Dr. Greig and the Downeys for their passion and zeal in developing the delightful, charming little dogs we have today. On the other hand, how better to keep the two major lines in existence because of these dedicated breeders, whatever the accusations? Credit must be given to John

Without the devotion and dedication of the early breeders, the Tibetan Terrier might have become a seldom-seen dog or have faded from existence as a breed.

The first Tibetan Terrier puppy was imported to the US in 1956, and like the Tibetan Terrier puppies today, his unusual looks and buoyant personality created an interest in this unique breed. This is Oreo owned by Toodie Connor, DVM.

and Constance Downey (Luneville)—who are still breeding Tibetan Terriers—for their efforts and perseverance in the establishment of the breed in England. Without their competition, which must have stimulated Dr. Greig to preserve her Lamleh line even into her advancing old age and illness, the Tibetan Terrier may have remained one of Britain's seldom seen rare breeds, although one wonders how these charmers could possibly escape notice.

Mr. Graham Newell, an Englishman and an internationally known judge and breeder of the famous Ch. Dokham Cavarodossi of Tintavon and his equally famous little sister Ch. Dokham La Calisto, discussed the last days of Dr. Greig when he came to New York to judge at the Westminster Kennel Club. Still fiercely independent, although ill herself, she was caring for her sister, who was totally bedridden. Sadly and ironically, the same people who were breeding the despised Luneville dogs, which she called "those crossbreeds," were the ones who were rallying around and helping her. Mr. Newell was spending every spare weekend at Dr. Greig's home, helping her with household and kennel duties, and taking care of her records. Her breeding was limited but she still would not place her dogs with her countrymen and was still shipping abroad. The last of her breeding arrived in the United States to Alice Murphy in the year of her death, 1972. Mrs. Alice Murphy died in 1976. Dr. Greig's name is synonymous with Tibetan Terriers. She fought to the end of her life for her beloved breed, her harsh criticism, her unreasonable demands, and her feuds notwithstanding. She will always be remembered in the breed.

TIBETAN TERRIERS IN THE UNITED STATES

After the first "official" Tibetan Terrier arrived in the United States, imported by Dr. and Mrs. Murphy, interest grew rapidly. The breeders largely responsible for present-day Tibetan Terriers in America must include Elizabeth and Joseph Cammarata, whose prefix was Kalyani. They had two dogs from Alice Murphy and two dogs were imported from the Downeys, named Luneville Princess Kim-Ba and Luneville Prince Kana, a litter brother to the famed English champion Luneville Prince Khan. A third bitch by the name of Luneville Princess Posa had been imported from England; she had several owners but

Imports from England and loyal American breeders are largely responsible for the success of the Tibetan Terrier in the US. Owners, Beverly and Ken Edmonds.

ended up with Joan Rinker in New York. Although the Cammaratas remained active only a few years, they were major contributors to the foundation of American-bred Tibetan Terriers.

Tom and Shirley Dickerson of Missouri became acquainted with the Cammaratas and expressed an interest in their dogs. Later Luneville Princess Kim-Ba went to live with the Dickersons. She was bred to Kamba Kim-Bu of Shahi Taj, and produced Ch. Kyirong's Maha Siddhi and Ch. Tafra's Maha Kyo-Go of Kyirong, a strong influence on present-day Tibetan Terriers. Interest was strong and a club was formed in the St. Louis area. A match was held annually, which attracted exhibitors throughout the country.

Dr. and Mrs. Francis Corcoran, who were living in Missouri at that time, were also attracted to these little dogs and obtained a bitch from the Cammaratas named Kalyani's Kala Yami (actually purchased from the Dickersons), who was the first Tibetan Terrier to earn an obedience degree. The Corcorans later moved to Maryland and imported a dog named Luneville Chubitang Kangri, CDX (Companion Dog Excellent), from the Downeys and established the Legspa Line.

On the East Coast, Alice and Bill Smith of Ipswich, Massachusetts, had imported from England a dog named Luneville Prince Kumara and had obtained a bitch from the Corcorans named Chubitang's Susan. Later they imported another dog from England named Ch. Dokham's Prin-Su's Caspar, who, after his show career was over, made news by jumping out of a second-story motel window and walking away unscathed. The Smiths chose their prefix "Prin-Su" from the names of their first two Tibetan Terriers.

In Middletown, Connecticut, Jane and George Reif imported several dogs from Dr. Greig in England, and they purchased a bitch from Alice Murphy. They bred to the Smith's import Ch. Dokham's Prin-Su's Caspar, thereby establishing their important Shaggar line found on many pedigrees today.

In the mid-1960s, Susan Mechem was teaching school in West Africa; upon completion of her contract, she decided to visit her uncle, an American diplomat in Kathmandu, before returning to the United States. There she met Miss Ann Rohrer, who was in government service and who owned a Tibetan Terrier. Miss Rohrer tracked down a Tibetan Terrier bitch that she sent to Angela Mulliner, a prominent English breeder under the Anjuman prefix. When Susan returned to Pennsylvania she obtained a Tibetan Terrier from Bill Walsh in Virginia and started her Kathmandu line.

William Walsh from Virginia was also an important breeder in the early years. His first Tibetan Terrier came from Alice Murphy. He had also acquired Luneville Princess Posa and Kalyani's Kim from the Cammaratas, who, because of other commitments, were reducing their stock. Kalyani's Kim was an important producer and is prominent on many pedigrees of present-day dogs. Mr. Walsh was heartbroken when Kalyani's Kim died of heartworm disease. He sent Luneville Princess Posa to Joan Rinker (Loki prefix) of New York and became inactive in the breed.

In Virginia, Ruth and Charles Tevis became active a little later, and because of their close friendship with Alice Murphy, who was in failing health, theirs was an extension of her line. Their breeding was limited and selective, and many important dogs have come down from their Karchen line, a prefix they selected after the purchase of Ch. Karchen Lamleh of Kalai from Alice Murphy.

At first, Tibetan Terriers were often confused with the Lhasa Apso, shown here, but soon distinguished themselves as a unique breed.

About the same time, Bob and Dorothy Chase of California became very active under the prefix "Kyi-Ra" and continued the Lamleh of Kalai line in their breeding program.

After Mrs. Murphy's death in 1976, Jocelyn Therrell inherited the Murphy dogs and the prefix Lamleh of Kala and continued breeding for several years.

Ed and Eileen Wilk of Maryland had become enchanted with a bitch that Beverly Luecke owned named Lu-Rog's Georgiana Pan-Dan Lha-Mo, and they finally persuaded Beverly to let them have her. They also had purchased a bitch from Sue Love named Granlee's Honey Kongjo. The Wilks then purchased from Bill Walsh a male named Ch.Tsa-Lhor of Shahi-Taj, and their Kontan line was founded, from which came the all-time top-winning male, Ch. Kontan Shazam and his litter brother Ch. Kontan's Kori-Nor-Ba-Tsa Lhor established another record when each won a Best in Show in the same weekend. No other Tibetan Terrier has equaled Shazam's record to date.

Also on the East Coast, not cast as breeders but playing an important role in the breed, Julian and Barbara Ross must be included as founders of breed recognition in the US, as it was through their efforts that records were kept that later were accepted without question by the American Kennel Club.

On the West Coast, Anne Keleman of Novato, California, cut out from a San Francisco newspaper a picture of a shaggy dog. The dog was owned by Dr. and Mrs. Francis Cocoran of Pebble Beach, California. A couple of years later, when she was ready for a dog, a letter was written to the Corcorans, who had by that time moved to Maryland. The Corcorans convinced her there was no breed like the Tibetan Terrier and thus another love affair with the breed was born. Anne later bought a seven-month-old puppy from Mrs. Neil Amend (Zim Sha prefix) in Washington state named Zim-Sha's Tasha Ti Song. The Amend children had named him Pi, short for Pirate, as he sported a black patch over one eye. He later became a well-known dog, traveling throughout the country and exhibiting in the AKC Miscellaneous Class. (The Miscellaneous Class is made up of breeds who are registered by the American Kennel Club but have not received recognition.) Pi was seen on television and numerous newspaper magazine articles were written about him. He loved the attention and became highly embarrassed when praised, stretching out his front legs and yawning deeply as if to say, "Aw shucks, it was nothing." He was America's first champion and the first Tibetan Terrier to place in the Non-Sporting Group. He was also the top-winning dog in the breed

Author Anne Keleman with AmCan. Int.Ch. Ryttergarden's Chocho, who obtained seven European titles before coming to the US.

In 1973. His show career was short-lived, as he was over seven years of age before the breed was recognized by the American Kennel Club. He was the foundation of Anne Keleman's Ti Song line, which was named after him.

Later Anne Keleman imported a world-renowned champion from Denmark who held seven European titles and had spent six months in quarantine in England and returned to his native home in Denmark. At about the same time, a letter was sent by Anne Keleman to his breeder-owner Jette Hansen, admiring this remarkable dog. Mrs. Hansen was in the process of moving to smaller quarters at the time and offered him for sale. Int. Ch. Ryttergarden's Chocho (known in England only as "Chocho") arrived in the

United States three months shy of his ninth birthday. Within five weeks he became an American and Canadian champion and ranked among the top-winning Tibetan Terriers in the country. He sired numerous champions, one of whom, Ch. Ti Song's J.P. Morgan of Tibeter, co-owned by the author, won the 1987 Tibetan Terrier National Specialty. He was over 16 years old when he died.

Later there were others who became active in the breed, but these were either extensions of the aforementioned lines or a combination of the lines.

More recently, imports have been arriving not only from England but from Denmark, Switzerland, Sweden, Finland and Germany. Most of these imports are of the combined Lamleh-Luneville lines, since there are few all-Lamleh breeders.

The early years in the United States were extremely frustrating to breeders and exhibitors. In spite of the fact that more and more interest was being generated in the breed, the Tibetan Terrier remained in the Miscellaneous Class at AKC shows from 1963 to 1973. In the late '60s and early '70s, interest had risen to a point where breeders and exhibitors were clamoring for recognition by the American Kennel Club. The Tibetan Terrier Club of America, Inc, which was headed by Alice Murphy, was being badgered to do something. Since membership in this club was by invitation only and consisted mainly of people who owned all-Lamleh dogs (a sharp division of opinion was also being displayed in America), the small group representing the membership was reluctant to push the American Kennel Club. The club also exercised a powerful hold on the breed and on the people who did not hold membership to the club. Many were contacting the American Kennel Club individually, imploring it to recognize the breed. Finally, the Tibetan Terrier Club of America, Inc. was contacted and it was suggested that membership be opened to all. The club was asked to bring the stud registry up to date with ILP (Indefinite Listing Privilege) numbers submitted which would later be changed into recognized AKC registration numbers.

On October 3, 1973, the Tibetan Terrier was shown as a fully recognized breed with its own classes. However, in 1973 the American Kennel Club had also recognized the Bichon Frise (who had spent only six months in Miscellaneous Class)

Ch. Ti-Song's J.P. Morgan, co-owned by the author, was the winner of the 1987 National Specialty Show.

and both breeds were placed in the Non-Sporting Group. The Bichons Frises made an immediate impact in the show ring and their look, distinctly different from any other breed, gained enthusiastic supporters from exhibitors and judges. They became a big hit and placed often in the Group.

Two new breeds in the Non-Sporting Group certainly was a disadvantage for the Tibetan Terrier. Judges were not enthused but confused. Those who had been charmed by the natural shaggy look of the breed now saw a different dog emerging from the show ring. Handlers had entered the picture, and coats were being straightened and sleeked down, and in some cases even ironed. There was a straight precision part down the back. The judges sometimes called them large Lhasa Apsos based on their appearance. One by one exhibitors capitulated and began presenting these naturally shaggy little dogs with straight parts from the nose down to the tip of the tail, groomed to the tee with coats hanging to the ground. The judges became convinced that indeed this was a distinct breed and some even became as enamored of them as their enthusiastic owners. Today, judges are giving Tibetan Terriers the same consideration as the other breeds in the Group. In England they were still being shown in their natural state. However, fads follow and they have become as fashionably groomed there as they are in the US.

REFLECTIONS ON THE TIBETAN TERRIER

San Francisco boasts a large Chinese population, and one of its largest celebrations is the Chinese New Year. The banners used in the 1982 Year of the Dog celebration included what was claimed to be the seven native Chinese breeds. They were: the Tibetan Terrier, the Pekingese, the Shar-Pei, the Shih Tzu, the Pug, the Chow Chow, the Tibetan Mastiff, and one simply called the Hairless. The banners, one of which the author was fortunate

These Tibetan Terriers go visiting with some of the 88 attendees at the annual "Tea Party" at the Presidio in San Francisco.

enough to obtain, also stated that the origin of the above-mentioned dogs traced back to ancient China, as far back as the Han and Tsang Dynasty, about 150 BC.

For centuries, according to the banner, the royal family used these dogs as companions and pets and treated them as members of the family. Notably absent from the list are the Lhasa Apso and Tibetan Spaniel. If this is true—and how can we dispute their claim—then the Tibetan Terrier and the Tibetan Mastiff somehow made their way from China into Tibet, instead of vice versa. If it is also true that only males were sent as gifts to China from Tibet, where did the females come from to perpetuate the breed in China? The mystery may never be solved.

In a pamphlet released in 1970, a group of judges, all of whom had owned and bred dogs in

Tibet, discussed and recorded their definitions and comments on the various breeds of Tibetan dogs at the first Tibetan Apso show held in New Delhi. They claimed the Apsos made their appearance in Mongolia around the time of Genghis Khan (1167-1227) and in China during the reign of Kublai Khan (1215-1294) and the Manchu Emperors (1115-1234). Here we have a conflict of dates, since the Chinese banners mentioned previously dated the Tibetan Terrier to the Han and Tsang Dynasty at about 150 BC. This group of judges also stated that the Apso ("hairy ones") found their way into Russia at about this time. Since we do not know the history of the Tibetan Terrier in Russia, this may be the reason we know there are Tibetan Terriers in Russia and also a larger dog with a physical resemblance to the Tibetan Terrier.

This adorable Tibetan Terrier pup is Brendan owned by Toodie Connor, DVM.

This group of judges classified the dogs into three different types. Type I, "Pet Dogs," was broken down into five classes. These dogs were slightly smaller than the Tibetan Terrier, but included the Tibetan Spaniel. Type II was "Mastiffs," with three categories, and included the Tibetan Terrier, called "Dhokhi Apso" ("Dhokhi" means outdoor dog). Type III was the Shaki. This was a distinct breed used for hunting similar to the Alaskan Malamute. Since this discussion was mainly on the subject of the Lhasa Apso, it dealt only briefly with the Tibetan Terrier as mentioned above. Why they were classified with the Mastiffs is unclear. Perhaps there was no other category into which they could fit, as the Tibetan Spaniel was also included under "Mastiffs" as well as "Pet Dogs." It must be remembered that this breed was known as the "Tibetan Terrier" only in the western world and in India, where it was named.

LUNEVILLE AND KALAI OF LAMLEH LINES

Almost certainly anyone interested in the Tibetan Terrier will be confronted by the issue of the two predominant pedigree lines. In a study of the pedigrees of the first 45 Tibetan Terriers imported into the United States from a booklet released by the Tibetan Terrier Club of America, Inc. in the early 1970s, it was found that almost without exception they contained dogs of unknown origins. These dogs were Lady Tow-Sa, Princess Chan, Ukie and Audrey of Carolina, all of whom had been brought to England by people other than Dr. Greig. All of these dogs were bred into Dr. Grieg's line. The two dogs whose pedigrees could not be traced to the above-mentioned dogs of unknown origin were Kalai of Lamleh, retained by Mrs. Alice Murphy to establish her Kalai of Lamleh and bred to Gremlin Cortina, the first "official" Tibetan Terrier, and Kalyani of Lamleh, who was sent to the Cammaratas in Missouri and was the foundation of the Kalyani and Kyirong lines. It must be noted that Gremlin Cortina's pedigree includes Lady Tow-Sa, whose parents were of unknown origin. A bitch later acquired by Mrs. Murphy also included Nin-Ty of Lamleh, who had two ancestors of unknown origin, one of which was Ukie, which had been bred into Dr. Greig's Lamleh line. This contradicts the "pure" Lamleh pedigrees.

LIVING WITH A TIBETAN TERRIER

No one really "owns" a Tibetan Terrier. They are charming little creatures with engaging personalities that they use to the limit. One must assume that the primary function of the Tibetan Terrier in Tibet was not just as a companion—he had to earn his keep. He is reported to be the foundation of the Puli (Hungarian Sheepdog), which is known as one of the most intelligent dogs in the world. He is one of the best guard dogs in existence. He is a natural retriever. He will sit at a gopher hole for hours without moving, waiting for the little fellow to pop his head out of the hole. Tibetan Terriers have been seen pointing and

Although he may look like a big "couch potato," the Tibetan Terrier is actually a very alert and active dog with excellent protective instincts. Owner, Bonnie Brock.

flushing birds. Their ability to scale deep slopes is outstanding, and there have been pictures of them sitting on fences and in trees, which must certainly reflect their native heritage.

The climate, the terrain, the harsh living conditions and the never-ending search for food in Tibet made him "the dog for all reasons." Now we put companionship at the top of the list. Here is where the Tibetan Terrier shines. He is a family dog. He wants to be with

The Tibetan Terrier is a generally long-lived, healthy breed who loves to be around his family. Ch. Bel Fluer of Tamridge at 14 years of age.

you. Your home is *his* castle. Everything becomes his own—the house, the yard, and especially the car. The car is his very own and he permits you to chauffeur him about. He loves to travel (due to his heritage?). He wants to know what you are doing and why you are doing it. He can be extremely stubborn and will tax you to the limit at times. He is best handled with persuasion, not punishment. He is not a dog to sit in the backyard, although he adapts to your schedule. He loves companionship, both animal and human. He is a born clown and a traffic stopper.

Although he is a healthy dog with a life span of 14 to 16 years, he is not exempt from some of the same afflictions that affect other breeds. Cases of hip dysplasia, hernias, subluxated patellas, progressive retinal atrophy and lens luxation have occurred, and dedicated breeders are selective in planning their breedings. These dogs can be extremely sensitive to fleas and susceptible to skin irritations caused by fleas.

GROOMING A TIBETAN TERRIER

The adult Tibetan Terrier's coat is comparable to human hair. A weekly brushing is necessary and the tools of the trade are a pin brush, a slicker brush and a comb. The easiest way to groom the Tibetan Terrier is to teach him in the beginning to lie on his side. He will object to the first two or three times, but be firm and place your arm on him to hold him down. As the dog becomes accustomed to being brushed in this manner, you might even hear a gentle snore or two. Start at the tail and draw imaginary one-inch lines from the top of his back straight down to the bottom, whether you are doing back legs or stomach or shoulders.

Beginning at an early age, a regular grooming regimen is a great way to keep abreast of any health problems your Tibetan may have, as well as a way to spend relaxing quality time with your dog. Owner, Linda Tyras.

Brush this one-inch line with your pin brush the way the hair grows and don't move on until every hair is standing out with no sign of mats. If you find a mat, gently brush with a slicker brush until it is free. Brush the entire side of the dog, leaving the bottom of the back legs free. When you are finished, flip the dog over to the other side and follow the same procedure.

You may now go back and brush the legs with a slicker brush by holding the leg in one hand and brushing with the other. Stand the dog up and brush the coat down, then comb with a good steel comb to see if you have missed any spots. He is now ready for his bath.

Use a good shampoo or a flea shampoo in those areas where fleas are prevalent. Wet the coat thoroughly. This may take some time as Tibetan Terrier coats resist water. Apply the shampoo and wash the entire dog. A good sponge will distribute the soap properly. Rinse well and apply the second portion of shampoo. The second shampoo will polish the hair and make it shine. Rinse thoroughly and, when you have finished, rinse again. A conditioner may be applied at this point or a vinegar rinse of mild solution. Most pet owners have their own favorite finishing touches.

Rinse off again and you are ready to dry. You can find shampoos and conditioners at your favorite pet shop. If you have taught your dog to lie on his side, he can easily be brush-dried with a blow dryer. Proceed in the same manner as you did when brushing him. On a warm sunny day, brush him dry outside.

Opposite: The Tibetan Terrier's long, thick coat needs daily grooming to keep it looking its best. Ch. Rje-Bo's Decatur's Clairmont owned by Beverly and Ken Edmonds.

Use a steel comb to groom the hair around your Tibetan's face, as well as to remove any mats or tangles.

YOUR PUPPY'S NEW HOME

Before actually collecting your puppy, it is better that you purchase the basic items you will need in advance of the pup's arrival date. This allows you more opportunity to shop around and ensure you have exactly what you want rather than having to buy lesser quality in a hurry.

It is always better to collect the puppy as early in the day as possible. In most instances this will mean that

the puppy has a few hours with your family before it is time to retire for his first night's sleep away from his former home.

If the breeder is local, then you may not need any form of box to place the puppy in when you bring him home. A member of the family can hold the pup in his lap—duly protected by some towels just in case the puppy becomes car sick! Be sure to advise the breeder at what time you hope to arrive for the puppy, as this will obviously influence the feeding of the pup that morning or afternoon. If you arrive early in the

A little puppy is a big responsibility! Once you bring your new Tibetan Terrier puppy home, he will depend on you for everything. Owner, Elissa Hirsch.

Tibetan Terriers love to ride in the car, so provide your dog with a safe crate to travel in when you hit the road.

day, then they will likely only give the pup a light breakfast so as to reduce the risk of travel sickness.

If the trip will be of a few hours duration, you should take a travel crate with you. The crate will provide your pup with a safe place to lie down and rest during the trip. During the trip, the puppy will no doubt wish to relieve his bowels, so you will have to make a few stops. On a long journey you may need a rest yourself, and can take the opportunity to let the puppy get some fresh air. However, do not let the puppy walk where there may have been a lot of other dogs because he might pick up an infection. Also, if he relieves his bowels at such a time, do not just leave the feces where they were dropped. This is the height of irre-sponsibility. It has resulted in many public parks and other places actually banning dogs. You can pur-chase poop-scoops from your pet shop and should have them with you whenever you are taking the dog out where he might foul a public place.

Your journey home should be made as quickly as possible. If it is a hot day, be sure the car interior is amply supplied with fresh air. It should never be too hot or too cold for the puppy. The pup must never be placed where he might be subject to a draft. If the journey requires an overnight stop at a motel, be aware that other guests will not appreciate a puppy crying half the night. You must regard the puppy as a baby and comfort him so he does not cry for long periods. The worst thing you can do is to shout at or smack him. This will mean your relationship is off to a really bad start. You wouldn't smack a baby, and your puppy is still very much just this.

ON ARRIVING HOME

By the time you arrive home the puppy may be very tired, in which case he should be taken to his sleeping area and allowed to rest. Children should not be allowed to interfere with the pup when he is sleeping. If the pup is not tired, he can be allowed to investigate his new home—but always under your close supervision. After a short look around, the puppy will no doubt appreciate a light meal and a drink of water. Do not overfeed him at his first meal because he will be in an excited state and more likely to be sick.

Although it is an obvious temptation, you should not invite friends and neighbors around to see the new arrival until he has had at least 48 hours in which to settle down. Indeed, if you can delay this longer then do so, especially if the puppy is not fully vaccinated. At the very least, the visitors might introduce some local bacteria on their clothing that the puppy is not immune to. This aspect is always a risk when a pup has been moved some distance, so the fewer people the pup meets in the first week or so the better.

Make sure you have a comfortable dog bed for your Tibetan Terriers to nap in. Furnish it with a soft blanket or pillow to make it extra cozy.

An open door is an invitation for danger and mischief, so be sure that all doors are secured and your puppy is always supervised when inside. Owner, Linda Tyras.

DANGERS IN THE HOME

Your home holds many potential dangers for a little mischievous puppy, so you must think about these in advance and be sure he is protected from them. The more obvious are as follows:

Open Fires. All open fires should be protected by a mesh screen guard so there is no danger of the pup being burned by spitting pieces of coal or wood.

Electrical Wires. Puppies just love chewing on things, so be sure that all electrical appliances are neatly hidden from view and are not left plugged in when not in use. It is not sufficient simply to turn the plug switch to the off position—pull the plug from the socket.

Open Doors. A door would seem a pretty innocuous object, yet with a strong draft it could kill or injure a puppy easily if it is slammed shut. Always ensure there is no risk of this happening. It is most likely during warm weather when you have windows or outside doors open and a sudden gust of wind blows through.

Balconies. If you live in a high-rise building, obviously the pup must be protected from falling. Be sure

37

The kitchen can be a dangerous place for a unsupervised dog. Always be extra careful when your Tibetan Terriers are around. Owners, John and Kathy Schaefer.

he cannot get through any railings on your patio, balcony, or deck.

Ponds and Pools. A garden pond or a swimming pool is a very dangerous place for a little puppy to be near. Be sure it is well screened so there is no risk of the pup falling in. It takes barely a minute for a pup—or a child—to drown.

The Kitchen. While many puppies will be kept in the kitchen, at least while they are toddlers and not able to control their bowel movements, this is a room full of danger—especially while you are cooking. When cooking, keep the puppy in a play pen or in another room where he is safely out of harm's way. Alternatively, if you have a carry box or crate, put him in this so he can still see you but is well protected.

Be aware, when using washing machines, that more than one puppy has clambered in and decided to have a nap and received a wash instead! If you leave the washing machine door open and leave the room for any reason, then be sure to check inside the machine before you close the door and switch on.

Small Children. Toddlers and small children should never be left unsupervised with puppies. In spite of such advice it is amazing just how many people not only do this but also allow children to pull and maul pups. They should be taught from the outset that a puppy is not a plaything to be dragged about the home—and they should be promptly scolded if they disobey.

Children must be shown how to lift a puppy so it is safe. Failure by you to correctly educate your children about dogs could one day result in their getting a very nasty bite or scratch. When a puppy is lifted, his weight must always be supported. To lift the pup, first place your right hand under his chest. Next, secure the pup by using your left hand to hold his neck. Now you can lift him and bring him close to your chest. Never lift a pup by his ears and, while he can be lifted by the scruff of his neck where the fur is loose, there is no reason ever to do this, so don't.

Tibetans and children love each other's company. Dog ownership can teach a child a lot about responsibility and life.

Beyond the dangers already cited you may be able to think of other ones that are specific to your home—steep basement steps or the like. Go around your home and check out all potential problems—you'll be glad you did.

THE FIRST NIGHT

The first few nights a puppy spends away from his mother and littermates are quite traumatic for him. He will feel very lonely, maybe cold, and will certainly miss the heartbeat of his siblings when sleeping. To help overcome his loneliness it may help to place a clock next to his bed—one with a loud tick. This will in some way soothe him, as the clock ticks to a rhythm not dissimilar from a heart beat. A cuddly toy may also help in the first few weeks. A dim nightlight may provide some comfort to the puppy, because his eyes will not yet be fully able to see in the dark. The puppy may want to leave his bed for a drink or to relieve himself.

If the pup does whimper in the night, there are two things you should not do. One is to get up and chastise him, because he will not understand why you are shouting at him; and the other is to rush to comfort him every time he cries because he will quickly realize that if he wants you to come running all he needs to do is to holler loud enough!

On his first night in his new home, your Tibetan puppy may miss the company of his dam and littermates. Pay him extra attention during this lonely time.

By all means give your puppy some extra attention on his first night, but after this quickly refrain from so doing. The pup will cry for a while but then settle down and go to sleep. Some pups are, of course, worse than others in this respect, so you must use balanced judgment in the matter. Many owners take their pups to bed with them, and there is certainly nothing wrong with this.

The pup will be no trouble in such cases. However, you should only do this if you intend to let this be a permanent arrangement, otherwise it is hardly fair to the puppy. If you have decided to have two puppies, then they will keep each other company and you will have few problems.

Tibetans are extremely friendly and get along wonderfully with other Tibetans as well as other pets. These guys look like one big happy family!

OTHER PETS

If you have other pets in the home then the puppy must be introduced to them under careful supervision. Puppies will get on just fine with any other pets—but you must make due allowance for the respective sizes of the pets concerned, and appreciate that your puppy has a rather playful nature. It would be very foolish to leave him with a young rabbit. The pup will want to play and might bite the bunny and get altogether too rough with it. Kittens are more able to defend themselves from overly cheeky pups, who will get a quick scratch if they overstep the mark. The adult cat could obviously give the pup a very bad

scratch, though generally cats will jump clear of pups and watch them from a suitable vantage point. Eventually they will meet at ground level where the cat will quickly hiss and box a puppy's ears. The pup will soon learn to respect an adult cat; thereafter they will probably develop into great friends as the pup matures into an adult dog.

HOUSETRAINING

Undoubtedly, the first form of training your puppy will undergo is in respect to his toilet habits. To achieve this you can use either newspaper, or a large litter tray filled with soil or lined with newspaper. A puppy cannot control his bowels until he is a few months old, and not fully until he is an adult. Therefore you must anticipate his needs and be prepared for a few accidents. The prime times a pup will urinate and defecate are shortly after he wakes up from a sleep, shortly after he has eaten, and after he has been playing awhile. He will usually whimper and start searching the room for a suitable place. You must quickly pick him up and place him on the newspaper or in the litter tray. Hold him in position gently but firmly. He might jump out of the box without doing anything on the first one or two occasions, but if you simply repeat the procedure every time you think he wants to relieve himself then eventually he will get the message.

If you already have another dog in the house, make sure your properly introduce him to your new Tibetan puppy. Murphy, a Newfoundland, meets his new eight-week-old Tibetan roommate.

Opposite: Paper training is an acceptable way to housetrain your puppy. Eventually, the puppy will just use one area of the paper and you can move the paper closer to the door and then outside.

When he does defecate as required, give him plenty of praise, telling him what a good puppy he is. The litter tray or newspaper must, of course, be cleaned or replaced after each use—puppies do not like using a dirty toilet any more than you do. The pup's toilet can be placed near the kitchen door and as he gets older the tray can be placed outside while the door is open. The pup will then start to use it while he is outside. From that time on, it is easy to get the pup to use a given area of the yard.

Many breeders recommend the popular alternative of crate training. Upon bringing the pup home, introduce him to his crate. The open wire crate is the best choice, placed in a restricted, draft-free area of the home. Put the pup's Nylabone® and other favorite toys in the crate along with a wool blanket or other suitable bedding. The puppy's natural cleanliness instincts prohibit him from soiling in the place where he sleeps, his crate. The puppy should be allowed to go in and out of the open crate during the day, but he should sleep in the crate at the night and at other intervals during the day. Whenever the pup is taken out of his crate, he should be brought outside (or to his newspapers) to do his business. Never use the crate as a place of punishment. You will see how quickly your pup takes to his crate, considering it as his own safe haven from the big world around him.

Line your Tibetan puppy's crate with a soft blanket and give him a treat when he goes inside. He will soon consider it his home. Owner, Linda Tyras.

THE EARLY DAYS

You will no doubt be given much advice on how to bring up your puppy. This will come from dog-owning friends, neighbors, and through articles and books you may read on the subject. Some of the advice will be sound, some will be nothing short of rubbish. What you should do above all else is to keep an open mind and let common sense prevail over prejudice and worn-out ideas that have been handed down over the centuries. There is no one way that is superior to all others, no more than there is no one dog that is exactly a replica of another. Each is an individual and must always be regarded as such.

Your Tibetan puppy will be very curious about the world around him and may be easily distracted when outside. Always supervise him closely when outdoors.

A dog never becomes disobedient, unruly, or a menace to society without the full consent of his owner. Your puppy may have many limitations, but the singular biggest limitation he is confronted with in so many instances is his owner's inability to understand his needs and how to cope with them.

IDENTIFICATION

It is a sad reflection on our society that the number of dogs and cats stolen every year runs into many thousands. To these can be added the number that get lost. If you do not want your cherished pet to be lost or stolen, then you should see that he is carrying a permanent identification number, as well as a temporary tag on his collar.

Permanent markings come in the form of tattoos placed either inside the pup's ear flap, or on the inner side of a pup's upper rear leg. The number given is then recorded with one of the national registration companies. Research laboratories will not purchase dogs carrying numbers as they realize these are clearly someone's pet, and not abandoned animals. As a result, thieves will normally abandon dogs so marked and this at least gives the dog a chance to be taken to the police or the dog pound, when the number can be traced and the dog reunited with its family. The only problem with this method at this time is that there are a number of registration bodies, so it is not always apparent which one the dog is registered with (as you provide the actual number). However, each registration body is aware of his competitors and will normally be happy to supply their addresses. Those holding the dog can check out which one you are with. It is not a perfect system, but until such is developed it's the best available.

A temporary tag takes the form of a metal or plastic disk large enough for you to place the dog's name and your phone number on it—maybe even your address as well. In virtually all places you will be required to obtain a license for your puppy. This may not become applicable until the pup is six months old, but it might apply regardless of his age. Much depends upon the state within a country, or the country itself, so check with your veterinarian if the breeder has not already advised you on this.

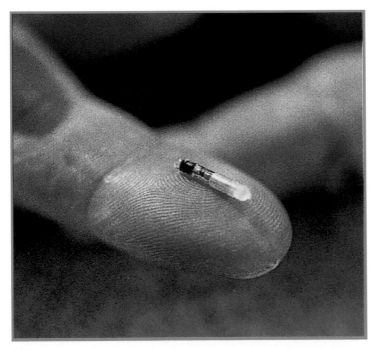

The newest method of identification is the microchip, a computer chip that is no bigger than a grain of rice, that is injected into the dog's skin.

FEEDING YOUR TIBETAN TERRIER

Dog owners today are fortunate in that they live in an age when considerable cash has been invested in the study of canine nutritional requirements. This means dog food manufacturers are very concerned about ensuring that their foods are of the best quality. The result of all of their studies, apart from the food itself, is that dog owners are bombarded

The breeder you obtain your puppy from should have started him on a nutritional, high-quality dog food. These four-week-old puppies give solid food a try.

with advertisements telling them why they must purchase a given brand. The number of products available to you is unlimited, so it is hardly surprising to find that dogs in general suffer from obesity and an excess of vitamins, rather than the reverse. Be sure to feed age-appropriate food—puppy food up to one year of age, adult food thereafter. Generally breeders recommend dry food supplemented by canned, if needed.

FACTORS AFFECTING NUTRITIONAL NEEDS

Activity Level. A dog that lives in a country environment and is able to exercise for long periods of the day will need more food than the same breed of dog living in an apartment and given little exercise.

47

Quality of the Food. Obviously the quality of food will affect the quantity required by a puppy. If the nutritional content of a food is low then the puppy will need more of it than if a better quality food was fed.

Balance of Nutrients and Vitamins. Feeding a puppy the correct balance of nutrients is not easy because the average person is not able to measure out ratios of one to another, so it is a case of trying to see that nothing is in excess. However, only tests, or your veterinarian, can be the source of reliable advice.

Genetic and Biological Variation. Apart from all of the other considerations, it should be remembered that each puppy is an individual. His genetic make-up will influence not only his physical characteristics but also his metabolic efficiency. This being so, two pups from the same litter can vary quite a bit in the amount of food they need to perform the same function under the same conditions. If you consider the potential combinations of all of these factors then you will see that pups of a given breed could vary quite a bit in the amount of food they will need. Before discussing feeding quantities it is valuable to know at least a little about the composition of food and its role in the body.

COMPOSITION AND ROLE OF FOOD

The main ingredients of food are protein, fats, and carbohydrates, each of which is needed in relatively

POPpups™ are 100% edible and enhanced with dog-friendly ingredients like liver, cheese, spinach, chicken, carrots, or potatoes. They contain no salt, sugar, alcohol, plastic or preservatives. You can even microwave a POPpup™ to turn into a huge crackly treat.

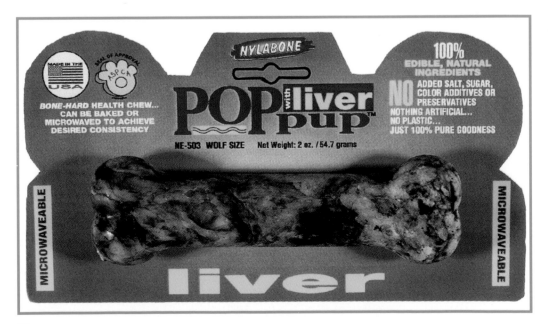

Carrots are rich in fiber, carbohydrates, and vitamin A. The Carrot Bone™ by Nylabone® is a durable chew containing no plastics or artificial ingredients and it can be served as-is, in a bone-hard form, or microwaved to a biscuit consistency.

large quantities when compared to the other needs of vitamins and minerals. The other vital ingredient of food is, of course, water. Although all foods obviously contain some of the basic ingredients needed for an animal to survive, they do not all contain the ingredients in the needed ratios or type. For example, there are many forms of protein, just as there are many types of carbohydrates. Both of these compounds are found in meat and in vegetable matter—but not all of those that are needed will be in one particular meat or vegetable. Plants, especially, do not contain certain amino acids that are required for the synthesis of certain proteins needed by dogs.

Likewise, vitamins are found in meats and vegetable matter, but vegetables are a richer source of most. Meat contains very little carbohydrates. Some vitamins can be synthesized by the dog, so do not need to be supplied via the food. Dogs are carnivores and this means their digestive tract has evolved to need a high quantity of meat as compared to humans. The digestive system of carnivores is unable to break down the tough cellulose walls of plant matter, but it is easily able to assimilate proteins from meat.

In order to gain its needed vegetable matter in a form that it can cope with, the carnivore eats all of its prey. This includes the partly digested food within the stomach. In commercially prepared foods, the cellulose is broken down by cooking. During this process the vitamin content is either greatly reduced or lost altogether. The manufacturer therefore adds vitamins once the heat process has been completed. This is why commercial foods are so useful as part of a feeding regimen, providing they are of good quality and from a company that has prepared the foods very carefully.

Proteins

These are made from amino acids, of which at least ten are essential if a puppy is to maintain healthy growth. Proteins provide the building blocks for the puppy's body. The richest sources are meat, fish and poultry, together with their by-products. The latter will include milk, cheese, yogurt, fishmeal, and eggs. Vegetable matter that has a high protein content includes soy beans, together with numerous corn and other plant extracts that have been dehydrated. The actual protein content needed in the diet will be determined both by the activity level of the dog and his age. The total protein need will also be influenced by the digestibility factor of the food given.

Fats

These serve numerous roles in the puppy's body. They provide insulation against the cold, and help

Roar-Hide® is completely edible and is high in protein (over 86%) and low in fat (less than one-third of 1%). Unlike common rawhide, it is safer, less messy, and more fun for your Tibetan Terrier.

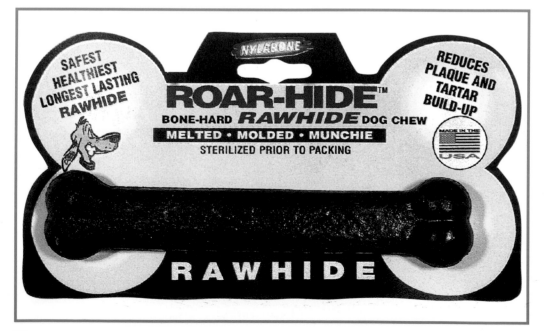

buffer the organs from knocks and general activity shocks. They provide the richest source of energy, and reserves of this, and they are vital in the transport of vitamins and other nutrients, via the blood, to all other organs. Finally, it is the fat content within a diet that gives it palatability. It is important that the fat content of a diet should not be excessive. This is because the high energy content of fats (more than twice that of protein or carbohydrate) will increase the overall energy content of the diet. The puppy will adjust its food intake to that of its energy needs, which are obviously more easily met in a high-

Puppies are full of boundless energy and need a well-balanced diet that will fit their activity levels and promote growth.

energy diet. This will mean that while the fats are providing the energy needs of the puppy, the over-all diet may not be providing its protein, vitamin, and mineral needs, so signs of protein deficiency will become apparent. Rich sources of fats are meat, their byproducts (butter, milk), and vegetable oils, such as safflower, olive, corn or soy bean.

Carbohydrates

These are the principal energy compounds given to puppies and adult dogs. Their inclusion within most commercial brand dog foods is for cost, rather than dietary needs. These compounds are more commonly known as sugars, and they are seen in simple or complex compounds of carbon, hydrogen, and oxygen. One of the simple sugars is called glucose, and it is vital

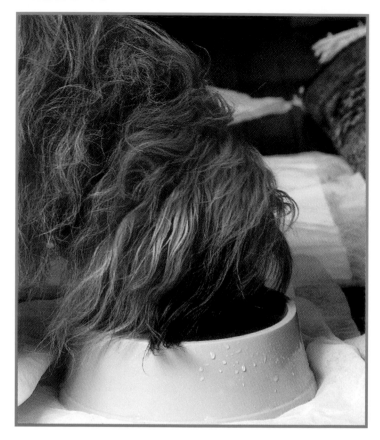

When your Tibetan Terrier is an adult, he will only need to be fed twice a day as long as he is getting all the nutrients he requires.

to many metabolic processes. When large chains of glucose are created, they form compound sugars. One of these is called glycogen, and it is found in the cells of animals. Another, called starch, is the material that is found in the cells of plants.

Vitamins

These are not foods as such but chemical compounds that assist in all aspects of an animal's life. They help in so many ways that to attempt to describe these effectively would require a chapter in itself. Fruits are a rich source of vitamins, as is the liver of most animals. Many vitamins are unstable and easily destroyed by light, heat, moisture, or rancidity. An excess of vitamins, especially A and D, has been proven to be very harmful. Provided a puppy is receiving a balanced diet, it is most unlikely there will be a deficiency, whereas hypervitaminosis (an excess of vitamins) has become quite common due to owners and breeders feeding unneeded supplements. The only time you should feed extra vitamins to your puppy is if your veterinarian advises you to.

Minerals

These provide strength to bone and cell tissue, as well as assist in many metabolic processes. Examples are calcium, phosphorous, copper, iron, magnesium, selenium, potassium, zinc, and sodium. The recommended amounts of all minerals in the diet has not been fully established. Calcium and phosphorous are known to be important, especially to puppies. They help in forming strong bone. As with vitamins, a mineral deficiency is most unlikely in pups given a good and varied diet. Again, an excess can create problems—this applying equally to calcium.

Make sure your Tibetan Terrier has plenty of cool clean water to drink at all times.

Water

This is the most important of all nutrients, as is easily shown by the fact that the adult dog is made up of about 60 percent water, the puppy containing an even higher percentage. Dogs must retain a water balance, which means that the total intake should be balanced by the total output. The intake comes either by direct input (the tap or its equivalent), plus water released when food is oxidized, known as metabolic water (remember that all foods contain the elements hydrogen and oxygen that recombine in the body to create water). A dog without adequate water will lose condition more rapidly than one depleted of food, a fact common to most animal species.

AMOUNT TO FEED

The best way to determine dietary requirements is by observing the puppy's general health and physical appearance. If he is well covered with flesh, shows good bone development and muscle, and is an active alert puppy, then his diet is fine. A puppy will consume about twice as much as an adult (of the same breed). You should ask the breeder of your puppy to show you the amounts fed to their pups and this will be a good starting point.

The puppy should eat his meal in about five to seven minutes. Any leftover food can be discarded or placed into the refrigerator until the next meal (but be sure it is thawed fully if your fridge is very cold).

If the puppy quickly devours its meal and is clearly still hungry, then you are not giving him enough food. If he eats readily but then begins to pick at it, or walks away leaving a quantity, then you are probably giving him too much food. Adjust this

Opposite: A complete and well-balanced diet will be evident in your Tibetan's shiny coat and overall healthy appearance. Owner, Dorothy Chase.

Promote constructive chewing by giving your Tibetan puppy a Nylabone® to gnaw on. It is a safe, durable chew toy that will help prevent tooth decay.

Your Tibetan Terrier might love "people food," but show him you love him by providing him with the well-balanced diet he needs to stay healthy.

at the next meal and you will quickly begin to appreciate what the correct amount is. If, over a number of weeks, the pup starts to look fat, then he is obviously overeating; the reverse is true if he starts to look thin compared with others of the same breed.

WHEN TO FEED

It really does not matter what times of the day the puppy is fed, as long as he receives the needed quantity of food. Puppies from 8 weeks to 12 or 16 weeks need 3 or 4 meals a day. Older puppies and adult dogs should be fed twice a day. What is most important is that the feeding times are reasonably regular. They can be tailored to fit in with your own timetable—for example, 7 a.m. and 6 p.m. The dog will then expect his meals at these times each day. Keeping regular feeding times and feeding set amounts will help you monitor your puppy's or dog's health. If a dog that's normally enthusiastic about mealtimes and eats readily suddenly shows a lack of interest in food, you'll know something's not right.

TRAINING YOUR TIBETAN TERRIER

The Tibetan Terrier is an intelligent dog that loves to please his master and is easily trainable. Maxwell has been trained to be a therapy dog and constant companion to his autistic friend Evan.

Once your puppy has settled into your home and responds to his name, then you can begin his basic training. Before giving advice on how you should go about doing this, two important points should be made. You should train the puppy in isolation of any potential distractions, and you should keep all lessons very short. It is essential that you have the full attention of your puppy. This is not possible if there are other people about, or televisions and radios on, or other pets in the vicinity. Even when the pup has become a young adult, the maximum time you should allocate to a lesson is about 20 minutes. However, you can give the puppy more than one lesson a day, three being as many as are recommended, each well spaced apart.

Before beginning a lesson, always play a little game with the puppy so he is in an active state of mind and thus more receptive to the matter at hand. Likewise, always end a lesson with fun-time for the pup,

and always—this is most important—end on a high note, praising the puppy. Let the lesson end when the pup has done as you require so he receives lots of fuss. This will really build his confidence.

COLLAR AND LEASH TRAINING

Training a puppy to his collar and leash is very easy. Place a collar on the puppy and, although he will initially try to bite at it, he will soon forget it, the more so if you play with him. You can leave the collar on for a few hours. Some people leave their dogs' collars on all of the time, others only when they are taking the dog out. If it is to be left on, purchase a narrow or round one so it does not mark the fur.

Once the puppy ignores his collar, then you can attach the leash to it and let the puppy pull this along behind it for a few minutes. However, if the pup starts to chew at the leash, simply hold the leash but keep it slack and let the pup go where he wants. The idea is to let him get the feel of the leash, but not get in the habit of chewing it. Repeat this a couple of times a day for two days and the pup will get used to the leash without thinking that it will restrain him—which you will not have attempted to do yet.

Teaching your Tibetan to wear his collar and leash is one of the first training tasks you will undertake together. Once he gets used to wearing it, he won't even know it's there.

Next, you can let the pup understand that the leash will restrict his movements. The first time he realizes this, he will pull and buck or just sit down. Immediately call the pup to you and give him lots of fuss. Never tug on the leash so the puppy is dragged along the floor, as this simply implants a negative thought in his mind.

A well-mannered Tibetan Terrier can accompany you anywhere and will make friends wherever he goes!

THE COME COMMAND

Come is the most vital of all commands and especially so for the independently minded dog. To teach

the puppy to come, let him reach the end of a long lead, then give the command and his name, gently pulling him toward you at the same time. As soon as he associates the word come with the action of moving toward you, pull only when he does not respond immediately. As he starts to come, move back to make him learn that he must come from a distance as well as when he is close to you. Soon you may be able to practice without a leash, but if he is slow to come or notably disobedient, go to him and pull him toward you, repeating the command. Never scold a dog during this exercise—or any other exercise. Remember the trick is that the puppy must want to come to you. For the very independent dog, hand signals may work better than verbal commands.

Teach your Tibetan Terrier hand signals in conjuction with verbal commands. This will come in handy if your dog is a great distance from you.

THE SIT COMMAND

As with most basic commands, your puppy will learn this one in just a few lessons. You can give the puppy two lessons a day on the sit command but he will make just as much progress with one 15-minute lesson each day. Some trainers will advise you that you should not proceed to other commands until the previous one has been learned really well. However, a bright young pup is quite capable of handling more than one command per lesson, and certainly per day. Indeed, as time progresses, you will be going through each command as a matter of routine before a new one is attempted. This is so the puppy always starts, as well as ends, a lesson on a high note, having successfully completed something.

Call the puppy to you and fuss over him. Place one hand on his hindquarters and the other under his upper chest. Say "Sit" in a pleasant (never harsh) voice. At the same time, push down his rear end and push up under his chest. Now lavish praise on the puppy. Repeat this a few times and your pet will get the idea. Once the puppy is in the sit position you will release your hands. At first he will tend to get up, so immediately repeat the exercise. The lesson will end when the pup is in the sit position. When the puppy understands the command, and does it right away, you can slowly move backwards so that you are a few feet away from him. If he attempts to come to you, simply place him back in the original position and start again. Do not attempt to keep the pup in the sit position for too long. At this age, even a few seconds is a long while and you do not want him to get bored with lessons before he has even begun them.

THE HEEL COMMAND

All dogs should be able to walk nicely on a leash without their owners being involved in a tug-of-war. The heel command will follow leash training. Heel training is best done where you have a wall to one side of you. This will restrict the puppy's lateral movements, so you only have to contend with forward and backward situations. A fence is an alternative, or you can do the lesson in the garage. Again, it is better to do the lesson in private, not on a public sidewalk where there will be many distractions.

With a puppy, there will be no need to use a choke collar as you can be just as effective with a regular one. The leash should be of good length, certainly not too short. You can adjust the space between you, the puppy, and the wall so your pet has only a small amount of room to move sideways. This being so, he will either hang back or pull ahead—the latter is the more desirable state as it indicates a bold pup who is not frightened of you.

Once your dog is housetrained, he will let you know when he needs to go outside. These two Tibetans wait patiently to go on their walk. Owners, John and Kathy Schaefer.

Hold the leash in your right hand and pass it through your left. As the puppy moves ahead and strains on the leash, give the leash a quick jerk backwards with your left hand, at the same time saying "Heel." The position you want the pup to be in is such that his chest is level with, or just behind, an imaginary line from your knee. When the puppy is in this position, praise him and begin walking again, and the whole exercise will be repeated. Once the puppy begins to get the message, you can use your left hand to pat the side of your knee so the pup is encouraged to keep close to your side.

It is useful to suddenly do an about-turn when the pup understands the basics. The puppy will now be behind you, so you can pat your knee and say "Heel." As soon as the pup is in the correct position, give him lots of praise. The puppy will now be beginning to associate certain words with certain actions. Whenever he is not in the heel position he will experience displeasure as you jerk the leash, but when he comes alongside you he will receive praise. Given these two options, he will always prefer the latter—assuming he has no other reason to fear you, which would then create a dilemma in his mind.

Once the lesson has been well learned, then you can adjust your pace from a slow walk to a quick one and the puppy will come to adjust. The slow walk is always the more difficult for most puppies, as they are usually anxious to be on the move.

If you have no wall to walk against then things will be a little more difficult because the pup will tend to wander to his left. This means you need to give lateral jerks as well as bring the pup to your side. End the lesson when the pup is walking nicely beside you. Begin the lesson with a few sit commands (which he understands by now), so you're starting with success and praise. If your puppy is nervous on the leash, you should never drag him to your side as you may see so many other people do (who obviously didn't invest in a good book like you did!). If the pup sits down, call him to your side and give lots of praise. The pup must always come to you because he wants to. If he is dragged to your side he will see you doing the dragging—a big negative. When he races ahead he does not see you jerk the leash, so all he knows is that something restricted his movement and, once he was in a given position, you gave him lots of praise. This is using canine psychology to your advantage.

Praise, attention and positive reinforcement are the best training motivators for your Tibetan Terrier.

Always try to remember that if a dog must be disciplined, then try not to let him associate the discipline with you. This is not possible in all matters but, where it is, this is definitely to be preferred.

THE STAY COMMAND

This command follows from the sit. Face the puppy and say "Sit." Now step backwards, and as you do, say "Stay." Let the pup remain in the position for only a few seconds before calling him to you and giving lots of praise. Repeat this, but step further back. You do not need to shout at the puppy. Your pet is not deaf; in fact, his hearing is far better than yours. Speak just loudly enough for the pup to hear, yet use a firm voice. You can stretch the word to form a "sta-a-a-y." If the pup gets up and comes to you simply lift him up, place

63

If you get your Tibetan Terrier used to his crate when he is young, crate training will be a snap!

him back in the original position, and start again. As the pup comes to understand the command, you can move further and further back.

The next test is to walk away after placing the pup. This will mean your back is to him, which will tempt him to follow you. Keep an eye over your shoulder, and the minute the pup starts to move, spin around and, using a sterner voice, say either "Sit" or "Stay." If the pup has gotten quite close to you, then, again, return him to the original position.

As the weeks go by you can increase the length of time the pup is left in the stay position—but two to three minutes is quite long enough for a puppy. If your puppy drops into a lying position and is clearly more comfortable, there is nothing wrong with this. Likewise, your pup will want to face the direction in which you walked off. Some trainers will insist that the dog faces the direction he was placed in, regardless of whether you move off on his blind side. I have never believed in this sort of obedience because it has no practical benefit.

THE DOWN COMMAND

From the puppy's viewpoint, the down command can be one of the more difficult ones to accept. This is because the position is one taken up by a submissive dog in a wild pack situation. A timid dog will roll over—a natural gesture of submission. A bolder pup will want to get up, and might back off, not feeling he should have to submit to this command. He will feel that he is under attack from you and about to be punished—which is what would be the position in his natural environment. Once he comes to understand this is not the case, he will accept this unnatural position without any problem.

You may notice that some dogs will sit very quickly, but will respond to the down command more slowly— it is their way of saying that they will obey the command, but under protest!

Your young Tibetan Terrier puppy will look to you, his owner, for the discipline and guidance he needs.

There two ways to teach this command. One is, in my mind, more intimidating than the other, but it is up to you to decide which one works best for you. The first method is to stand in front of your puppy and bring him to the sit position, with his collar and leash on. Pass the leash under your left foot so that when you pull on it, the result is that the pup's neck is forced downwards. With your free left hand, push the pup's shoulders down while at the same time saying "Down." This is when a bold pup will instantly try to back off and wriggle in full protest. Hold the pup firmly by the shoulders so he stays in the position for a second or two, then tell him what a good dog he is and give him lots of praise. Repeat this only a few times in a lesson because otherwise the puppy will get bored and upset over this command. End with an easy command that brings back the pup's confidence.

The second method, and the one I prefer, is done as follows: Stand in front of the pup and then tell him to sit. Now kneel down, which is immediately far less intimidating to the puppy than to have you towering above him. Take each of his front legs and pull them forward, at the same time saying "Down." Release the legs and quickly apply light pressure on the shoulders with your left hand. Then, as quickly, say "Good boy" and give lots of fuss. Repeat two or three times only. The pup will learn over a few lessons. Remember, this is a very submissive act on the pup's behalf, so there is no need to rush matters.

Working together at basic obedience will help keep your puppy out of trouble. This Tibetan Terrier is rearranging the shoe closet.

RECALL TO HEEL COMMAND

When your puppy is coming to the heel position from an off-leash situation—such as if he has been running free—he should do this in the correct manner. He should pass behind you and take up his position and then sit. To teach this command, have the pup in front of you in the sit position with his collar and leash on. Hold the leash in your right hand. Give him the command to heel, and pat your left knee. As the pup starts to move forward, use your right hand to guide him behind you. If need be you can hold his collar and walk the dog around the back of you to the desired position. You will need to repeat this a few times until the dog understands what is wanted.

When he has done this a number of times, you can try it without the collar and leash. If the pup comes up toward your left side, then bring him to the sit position in front of you, hold his collar and walk him around the back of you. He will eventually understand and automatically pass around your back each time. If the dog is already behind you when you recall him, then he should automatically come to your left side, which you will be patting with your hand.

THE NO COMMAND

This is a command that must be obeyed every time without fail. There are no halfway stages, he must be 100-percent reliable. Most delinquent dogs have never been taught this command; included in these are the jumpers, the barkers, and the biters. Were your puppy to approach a poisonous snake or any other potential danger, the no command, coupled with the recall, could save his life. You do not need to give a specific lesson for this command because it will crop up time and again in day-to-day life.

If the puppy is chewing a slipper, you should approach the pup, take hold of the slipper, and say "No" in a stern voice. If he jumps onto the furniture, lift him off and say "No" and place him gently on the floor. You must be consistent in the use of the command and apply it every time he is doing something you do not want him to do.

Once your puppy masters the basic commands, who knows how far he'll go? This Tibetan aspires to make it to the top!

YOUR HEALTHY TIBETAN TERRIER

Dogs, like all other animals, are capable of contracting problems and diseases that, in most cases, are easily avoided by sound husbandry—meaning well-bred and well-cared-for animals are less prone to developing diseases and problems than are carelessly bred and neglected animals. Your knowledge of how to avoid problems is far more valuable than all of the books and advice on how to cure them. Respectively, the only person you should listen to about treatment is your vet. Veterinarians don't have all the answers, but at least they are trained to analyze and treat illnesses, and are aware of the full implications of treatments. This does not mean a few old remedies aren't good standbys when all else fails, but in most cases modern science provides the best treatments for disease.

Opposite: Veterinarians are trained to analyze and treat illnesses. Having complete trust in your chosen veterinarian is tantamount to the long life of your dog.

PHYSICAL EXAMS

Your puppy should receive regular physical examinations or check-ups. These come in two forms. One is obviously performed by your vet, and the other is a day-to-day procedure that should be done by you. Apart from the fact the exam will highlight any problem at an early stage, it is an excellent way of socializing the pup to being handled.

To do the physical exam yourself, start at the head and work your way around the body. You are looking for any sign of lesions, or any indication of parasites on the pup. The most common parasites are fleas and ticks.

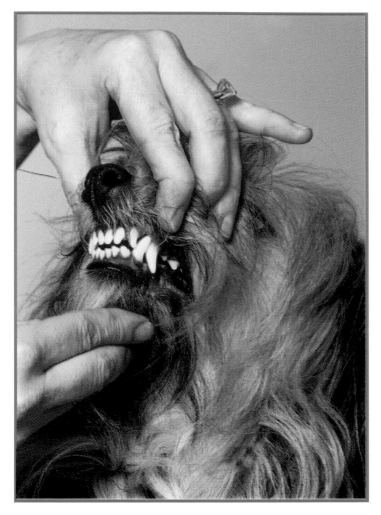

You should examine your Tibetan Terrier's mouth regularly to make sure there are no sores, foreign objects or tooth problems.

HEALTHY TEETH AND GUMS

Chewing is instinctual. Puppies chew so that their teeth and jaws grow strong and healthy as they develop. As the permanent teeth begin to emerge, it is painful and annoying to the puppy, and puppy owners must recognize that their new charges need something safe upon which to chew. Unfortunately, once the puppy's permanent teeth have emerged and settled solidly into the jaw, the chewing instinct does not fade. Adult dogs instinctively need to clean their teeth, massage their gums, and exercise their jaws through chewing.

It is necessary for your dog to have clean teeth. You should take your dog to the veterinarian at least once a year to have his teeth cleaned and to have his mouth examined for any sign of oral disease. Although dogs do not get cavities in the same way humans do, dogs'

The Hercules™ by Nylabone® has raised dental tips that help fight plaque on your Tibetan Terrier's teeth and gums.

teeth accumulate tartar, and more quickly than humans do! Veterinarians recommend brushing your dog's teeth daily. But who can find time to brush their dog's teeth daily? The accumulation of tartar and plaque on our dog's teeth when not removed can cause irritation and eventually erode the enamel and finally destroy the teeth. Advanced cases, while destroying the teeth, bring on gingivitis and periodontitis, two very serious conditions that can affect the dog's internal organs as well...to say nothing about bad breath!

Since everyone can't brush their dog's teeth daily or get to the veterinarian often enough for him to scale

Nylafloss® does wonders for your Tibetan Terrier's dental health by massaging his gums and literally flossing between his teeth, loosening plaque and tartar build-up. Unlike cotton tug toys, Nylafloss® won't rot or fray.

the dog's teeth, providing the dog with something safe to chew on will help maintain oral hygiene. Chew devices from Nylabone® keep dogs' teeth clean, but they also provide an excellent resource for entertainment and relief of doggie tensions. Nylabone® products give your dog something to do for an hour or two every day and during that hour or two, your dog will be taking an active part in keeping his teeth and gums healthy…without even realizing it! That's invaluable to your dog, and valuable to you!

Nylabone® provides fun bones, challenging bones, and *safe* bones. It is an owner's responsibility to recognize safe chew toys from dangerous ones. Your dog will chew and devour anything you give him. Dogs must not be permitted to chew on items that they can break. Pieces of broken objects can do internal damage to a dog, besides ripping the dog's mouth. Cheap plastic or rubber toys can cause stoppage in the intestines; such stoppages are operable only if caught immediately.

The most obvious choices, in this case, may be the worst choice. Natural beef bones were not designed for chewing and cannot take too much pressure from the sides. Due to the abrasive nature of these bones, they should be offered most sparingly. Knuckle bones, though once very popular for dogs, can be easily

Nylabone® is the only plastic dog bone made of 100% virgin nylon, specially processed to create a tough, durable, completely safe bone.

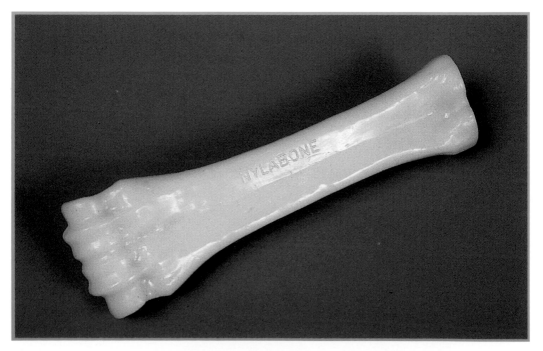

Chick-n-Cheez Chooz® are completely safe and nutritious health chews made from pure cheese protein, chicken, and fortified with vitamin E. They contain no salt, sugar, plastic, or preservatives and less than 1% fat.

chewed up and eaten by dogs. At the very least, digestion is interrupted; at worst, the dog can choke or suffer from intestinal blockage.

When a dog chews hard on a Nylabone®, little bristle-like projections appear on the surface of the bone. These help to clean the dog's teeth and add to the gum-massaging. Given the chemistry of the nylon, the bristle can pass through the dog's intestinal tract without effect. Since nylon is inert, no microorganism can grow on it, and it can be washed in soap and water or sterilized in boiling water or in an autoclave.

For the sake of your dog, his teeth and your own peace of mind, provide your dog with Nylabones®. They have 100 variations from which to choose.

FIGHTING FLEAS

Fleas are very mobile and may be red, black, or brown in color. The adults suck the blood of the host, while the larvae feed on the feces of the adults, which is rich in blood. Flea "dirt" may be seen on the pup as very tiny clusters of blackish specks that look like freshly ground pepper. The eggs of fleas may be laid on the puppy, though they are more commonly laid off the host in a favorable place, such as the bedding. They normally hatch in 4 to 21 days, depending on the temperature, but they can survive for up to 18 months if temperature conditions are not favorable. The larvae are maggot-like and molt a couple of times before forming pupae, which can survive long periods until the temperature, or the vibration of a nearby host, causes them to emerge and jump on a host.

There are a number of effective treatments available, and you should discuss them with your veterinarian, then follow all instructions for the one you choose. Any treatment will involve a product for your puppy or dog and one for the environment, and will require diligence on your part to treat all areas and thoroughly clean your home and yard until the infestation is eradicated.

THE TROUBLE WITH TICKS

Ticks are arthropods of the spider family, which means they have eight legs (though the larvae have six). They bury their headparts into the host and gorge on its blood. They are easily seen as small grain-like creatures sticking out from the skin. They are often picked up when dogs play in fields, but may also arrive in your yard via wild animals—even birds—or stray cats and dogs. Some ticks are species-specific, others are more adaptable and will host on many species.

The cat flea is the most common flea of dogs. It starts feeding soon after it makes contact with the dog.

The deer tick is the most common carrier of Lyme disease. Photo courtesy of Virbac Laboratories, Inc., Fort Worth, Texas.

The most troublesome type of tick is the deer tick, which spreads the deadly Lyme disease that can cripple a dog (or a person). Deer ticks are tiny and very hard to detect. Often, by the time they're big enough to notice, they've been feeding on the dog for a few days—long enough to do their damage. Lyme disease was named for the area of the United States in which it was first detected—Lyme, Connecticut—but has now been diagnosed in almost all parts of the U.S. Your veterinarian can advise you of the danger to your dog(s) in your area, and may suggest your dog be vaccinated for Lyme. Always go over your dog with a fine-toothed flea comb when you come in from walking through any area that may harbor deer ticks, and if your dog is acting unusually sluggish or sore, seek veterinary advice.

Attempts to pull a tick free will invariably leave the headpart in the pup, where it will die and cause an infected wound or abscess. The best way to remove ticks is to dab a strong saline solution, iodine, or alcohol on them. This will numb them, causing them to loosen their hold, at which time they can be removed with forceps. The wound can then be cleaned and covered with an antiseptic ointment. If ticks are common in your area, consult with your vet for a suitable pesticide to be used in kennels, on bedding, and on the puppy or dog.

INSECTS AND OTHER OUTDOOR DANGERS

There are many biting insects, such as mosquitoes, that can cause discomfort to a puppy. Many diseases are transmitted by the males of these species.

A pup can easily get a grass seed or thorn lodged between his pads or in the folds of his ears. These may go unnoticed until an abscess forms.

This is where your daily check of the puppy or dog will do a world of good. If your puppy has been playing in long grass or places where there may be thorns, pine needles, wild animals, or parasites, the check-up is a wise precaution.

SKIN DISORDERS

Apart from problems associated with lesions created by biting pests, a puppy may fall foul to a number of other skin disorders. Examples are ringworm, mange, and eczema. Ringworm is not caused by a worm, but is a fungal infection. It manifests itself as a sore-looking bald circle. If your puppy should have any form of bald patches, let your veterinarian check him over; a microscopic examination can confirm the condition. Many old remedies for ringworm exist, such as iodine, carbolic acid, formalin, and other tinctures, but modern drugs are superior.

Although your Tibetan Terrier loves spending time in the great outdoors, there may be dangers lurking in the grass, such as thorns and parasites. Always give your dog a thorough check-up after he has been playing outside.

Fungal infections can be very difficult to treat, and even more difficult to eradicate, because of the spores. These can withstand most treatments, other than burning, which is the best thing to do with bedding once the condition has been confirmed.

Mange is a general term that can be applied to many skin conditions where the hair falls out and a flaky crust develops and falls away.

Often, dogs will scratch themselves, and this invariably is worse than the original condition, for it opens lesions that are then subject to viral, fungal, or parasitic attack. The cause of the problem can be various species of mites. These either live on skin debris and the hair follicles, which they destroy, or they bury themselves just beneath the skin and feed on the tissue. Applying general remedies from pet stores is not recommended because it is essential to identify the type of mange before a specific treatment is effective.

Eczema is another non-specific term applied to many skin disorders. The condition can be brought about in many ways. Sunburn, chemicals, allergies to foods, drugs, pollens, and even stress can all produce a deterioration of the skin and coat. Given the range of causal factors, treatment can be difficult because the problem is one of identification. It is a case of taking each possibility at a time and trying to correctly diagnose the matter. If the cause is of a dietary nature then you must remove one item at a time in order to find out if the dog is allergic to a given food. It could, of course, be the lack of a nutrient that is the problem, so if the condition persists, you should consult your veterinarian.

INTERNAL DISORDERS

It cannot be overstressed that it is very foolish to attempt to diagnose an internal disorder without the advice of a veterinarian. Take a relatively common problem such as diarrhea. It might be caused by nothing more serious than the puppy hogging a lot of food or eating something that it has never previously eaten. Conversely, it could be the first indication of a potentially fatal disease. It's up to your veterinarian to make the correct diagnosis.

The following symptoms, especially if they accompany each other or are progressively added to earlier symptoms, mean you should visit the veterinarian right away:

Continual vomiting. All dogs vomit from time to time and this is not necessarily a sign of illness. They will eat grass to induce vomiting. It is a natural cleansing process common to many carnivores. However, continued vomiting is a clear sign of a problem. It may be a blockage in the pup's intestinal tract, it may be induced by worms, or it could be due to any number of diseases.

Diarrhea. This, too, may be nothing more than a temporary condition due to many factors. Even a change of home can induce diarrhea, because this often stresses the pup, and invariably there is some change in the diet. If it persists more than 48 hours then something is amiss. If blood is seen in the feces, waste no time at all in taking the dog to the vet.

Running eyes and/or nose. A pup might have a chill and this will cause the eyes and nose to weep. Again, this should quickly clear up if the puppy is placed in a warm environment and away from any drafts. If it does not, and especially if a mucous discharge is seen, then the pup has an illness that must be diagnosed.

Coughing. Prolonged coughing is a sign of a problem, usually of a respiratory nature.

Wheezing. If the pup has difficulty breathing and makes a wheezing sound when breathing, then something is wrong.

Cries when attempting to defecate or urinate. This might only be a minor problem due to the hard state of the feces, but it could be more serious, especially if the pup cries when urinating.

Cries when touched. Obviously, if you do not handle a puppy with care he might yelp. However, if he cries even when lifted gently, then he has an internal problem that becomes apparent when pressure is applied to a given area of the body. Clearly, this must be diagnosed.

Refuses food. Generally, puppies and dogs are greedy creatures when it comes to feeding time. Some might be more fussy, but none should refuse more than one meal. If they go for a number of hours without showing any interest in their food, then something is not as it should be.

General listlessness. All puppies have their off days when they do not seem their usual cheeky, mischievous selves. If this condition persists for more than two days then there is little doubt of a problem. They may not show any of the signs listed, other than perhaps a reduced interest in their food. There are many diseases that can develop internally without displaying obvious clinical signs. Blood, fecal, and other tests are needed in order to identify the disorder before it reaches an advanced state that may not be treatable.

WORMS

There are many species of worms, and a number of these live in the tissues of dogs and most other animals. Many create no problem at all, so you are not even aware they exist. Others can be tolerated in small levels, but become a major problem if they number more than a few. The most common types seen in dogs are roundworms and tapeworms. While roundworms are the greater problem, tapeworms require an intermediate host so are more easily eradicated.

Roundworms are spaghetti-like worms that cause a pot-bellied appearance and dull coat, along with more severe symptoms, such as diarrhea and vomiting. Photo courtesy of Merck AgVet.

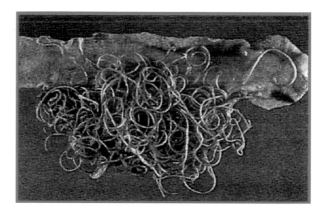

Roundworms of the species *Toxocara canis* infest the dog. They may grow to a length of 8 inches (20 cm) and look like strings of spaghetti. The worms feed on the digesting food in the pup's intestines. In chronic cases the puppy will become pot-bellied, have diarrhea, and will vomit. Eventually, he will stop eating, having passed through the stage when he always seems hungry. The worms lay eggs in the puppy and these pass out in his feces. They are then either ingested by the pup, or they are eaten by mice, rats, or beetles. These may then be eaten by the puppy and the life cycle is complete.

Larval worms can migrate to the womb of a pregnant bitch, or to her mammary glands, and this is how they pass to the puppy. The pregnant bitch can be wormed, which will help. The pups can, and should,

Whipworms are hard to find unless you strain your dog's feces, and this is best left to a veterinarian. Pictured here are adult whipworms.

be wormed when they are about two weeks old. Repeat worming every 10 to 14 days and the parasites should be removed. Worms can be extremely dangerous to young puppies, so you should be sure the pup is wormed as a matter of routine.

Tapeworms can be seen as tiny rice-like eggs sticking to the puppy's or dog's anus. They are less destructive, but still undesirable. The eggs are eaten by mice, fleas, rabbits, and other animals that serve as intermediate hosts. They develop into a larval stage and the host must be eaten by the dog in order to complete the chain. Your vet will supply a suitable remedy if tapeworms are seen or suspected. There are other worms, such as hookworms and whipworms, that are also blood suckers. They will make a pup anemic, and blood might be seen in the feces, which can be examined by the vet to confirm their presence. Cleanliness in all matters is the best preventative measure for all worms.

Heartworm infestation in dogs is passed by mosquitoes but can be prevented by a monthly (or daily) treatment that is given orally. Talk to your vet about the risk of heartworm in your area.

BLOAT (GASTRIC DILATATION)

This condition has proved fatal in many dogs, especially large and deep-chested breeds, such as the Weimaraner and the Great Dane. However, any dog can get bloat. It is caused by swallowing air during exercise, food/water gulping or another strenuous task. As many believe, it is not the result of flatulence. The stomach of an affected dog twists, disallowing food and blood flow and resulting in harmful toxins being released into the bloodstream. Death can easily follow if the condition goes undetected.

The best preventative measure is not to feed large meals or exercise your puppy or dog immediately after he has eaten. Veterinarians recommend feeding three smaller meals per day in an elevated feeding rack, adding water to dry food to prevent gulping, and not offering water during mealtimes.

VACCINATIONS

Every puppy, purebred or mixed breed, should be vaccinated against the major canine diseases. These are distemper, leptospirosis, hepatitis, and canine parvovirus. Your puppy may have received a temporary vaccination against distemper before you purchased him, but be sure to ask the breeder to be sure.

The age at which vaccinations are given can vary, but will usually be when the pup is 8 to 12 weeks old. By this time any protection given to the pup by antibodies received from his mother via her initial milk feeds will be losing their strength.

Rely on your veterinarian for the most effectual vaccination schedule for your Tibetan Terrier puppy.

The puppy's immune system works on the basis that the white blood cells engulf and render harmless

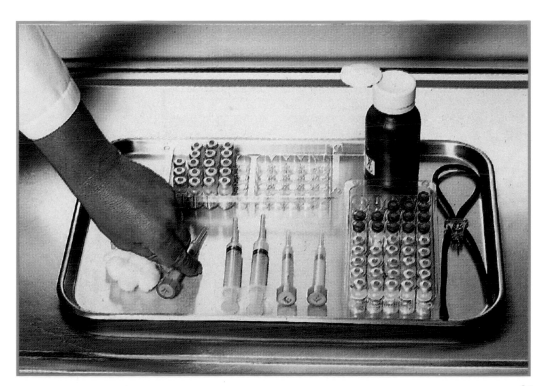

attacking bacteria. However, they must first recognize a potential enemy.

Vaccines are either dead bacteria or they are live, but in very small doses. Either type prompts the pup's defense system to attack them. When a large attack then comes (if it does), the immune system recognizes it and massive numbers of lymphocytes (white blood corpuscles) are mobilized to counter the attack. However, the ability of the cells to recognize these dangerous viruses can diminish over a period of time. It is therefore useful to provide annual reminders about the nature of the enemy. This is done by means of booster injections that keep the immune system on its alert. Immunization is not 100-percent guaranteed to be successful, but is very close. Certainly it is better than giving the puppy no protection.

Dogs are subject to other viral attacks, and if these are of a high-risk factor in your area, then your vet will suggest you have the puppy vaccinated against these as well.

Your puppy or dog should also be vaccinated against the deadly rabies virus. In fact, in many places it is illegal for your dog not to be vaccinated. This is to protect your dog, your family, and the rest of the animal population from this deadly virus that infects the nervous system and causes dementia and death.

ACCIDENTS

All puppies will get their share of bumps and bruises due to the rather energetic way they play. These will usually heal themselves over a few days. Small cuts should be bathed with a suitable disinfectant and then smeared with an antiseptic ointment. If a cut looks more serious, then stem the flow of blood with a towel or makeshift tourniquet and rush the pup to the veterinarian. Never apply so much pressure to the wound that it might restrict the flow of blood to the limb.

In the case of burns you should apply cold water or an ice pack to the surface. If the burn was due to a chemical, then this must be washed away with copious amounts of water. Apply petroleum jelly, or any vegetable oil, to the burn. Trim away the hair if need be. Wrap the dog in a blanket and rush him to the vet. The pup may go into shock, depending on the severity of the burn, and this will result in a lowered blood pressure, which is dangerous and the reason the pup must receive immediate veterinary attention.

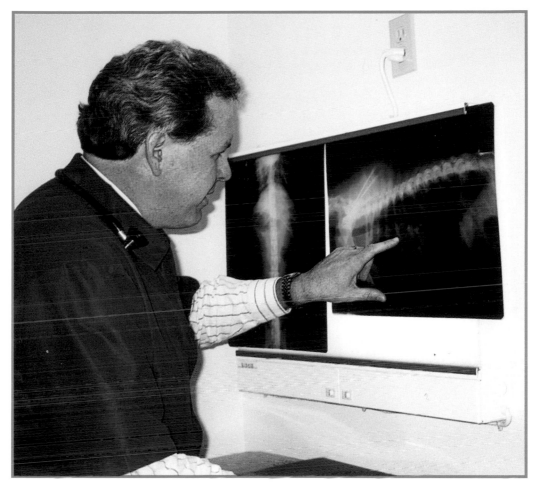

It is a good idea to x-ray the chest and abdomen on any dog hit by a car.

If a broken limb is suspected then try to keep the animal as still as possible. Wrap your pup or dog in a blanket to restrict movement and get him to the veterinarian as soon as possible. Do not move the dog's head so it is tilting backward, as this might result in blood entering the lungs.

Do not let your pup jump up and down from heights, as this can cause considerable shock to the joints. Like all youngsters, puppies do not know when enough is enough, so you must do all their thinking for them.

Provided you apply strict hygiene to all aspects of raising your puppy, and you make daily checks on his physical state, you have done as much as you can to safeguard him during his most vulnerable period. Routine visits to your veterinarian are also recommended, especially while the puppy is under one year of age. The vet may notice something that did not seem important to you.

CONGENITAL AND ACQUIRED DISORDERS

by Judy Iby, RVT

Veterinarians and breeders now recognize that many of the disease processes and faults in dogs, as well as in human beings, have a genetic predisposition. These faults are found not only in the purebred dog but in the mixed breed as well. Likely these diseases have been present for decades but more recently are being identified and attributed to inheritance. Fortunately many of these problems are not life threatening or even debilitating. Many of these disorders have a low incidence. It is true that some breeds and some bloodlines within a breed have a higher frequency than others. It is always wise to discuss this subject with breeders of your breed.

Presently very few of the hundreds of disorders can be identified through genetic testing. Hopefully with today's technology and the desire to improve our breeding stock, genetic testing will become more readily available. In the meantime the reputable breeder does the recommended testing for his breed. The American Kennel Club is encouraging OFA (Orthopedic Foundation for Animals) hip and elbow certification and CERF (Canine Eye Registration Foundation) certifications and is listing them on AKC registrations and pedigrees. This is a step forward for the AKC in encouraging better breeding. They also founded a Canine Health Foundation to aid in the research of diseases in the purebred dog.

Opposite: The responsible Tibetan Terrier breeder, understanding the potential problems within the breed, strives to produce healthy puppies and contribute to the betterment of the breed.

BONES AND JOINTS

Hip Dysplasia

Canine hip dysplasia has been confirmed in 79 breeds. It is the malformation of the hip joint's ball and socket, with clinical signs from none to severe hip lameness. It may appear as early as five months. The incidence is

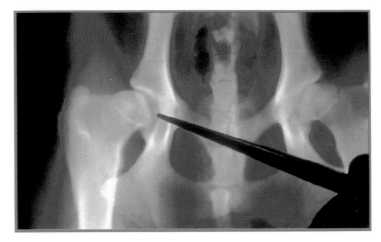

Radiograph of a dog with hip dysplasia. Note the flattened femoral head at the marker. Photo courtesy of Toronto Academy of Veterinary Medicine, Toronto, Canada.

reduced within a bloodline by breeding normal to normal, generation after generation. Upon submitting normal pelvic radiographs, the OFA will issue a certification number.

Elbow Dysplasia

Elbow dysplasia results from abnormal development of the ulna, one of the bones of the upper arm. During bone growth, a small area of bone (the anconeal process) fails to fuse with the rest of the bone. This results in an unstable elbow joint and lameness, which is aggravated by exercise. OFA certifies free of this disorder.

Patellar Luxation

This condition can be medial or lateral. Breeders call patellar luxations "slips" for "slipped kneecaps." OFA offers a registry for this disorder. Patellar luxations may or may not cause problems.

Intervertebral Disk Disease (IVD)

IVD is a condition in which a disk(s), the cushion between each vertebrae of the spine, tears and the gel-like material leaks out and presses on the spinal cord. The degeneration is progressive, starting as early as two to nine months, but usually the neurological symptoms are not apparent until three to six years of age. Symptoms include pain, paresis (weariness), incoordination, and paralysis. IVD is a medical emergency. If you are unable to get professional care immediately, then confine your dog to a crate or small area until he can be seen.

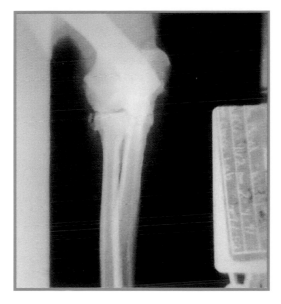

Fragmented coronoid process of the elbow, a manifestation of elbow dysplasia. Photo courtesy of Jack Henry.

Spondylitis

Usually seen in middle to old-age dogs and potentially quite serious in the latter, spondylitis is inflammation of the vertebral joints and degeneration of intervertebral disks resulting in bony spur-like outgrowths that may fuse.

CARDIOVASCULAR AND LYMPHATIC SYSTEMS

Dilated Cardiomyopathy

Prevalent in several breeds, this is a disease in which the heart muscle is damaged or destroyed to the point that it cannot pump blood properly through the body resulting in signs of heart failure. Diagnosis is confirmed by cardiac ultrasound.

Lymphosarcoma

This condition can occur in young dogs but usually appears in dogs over the age of five years. Symptoms include fever, weight loss, anorexia, painless enlargement of the lymph nodes, and nonspecific signs of illness. It is the most common type of cancer found in dogs. Chemotherapy treatment will prolong the dog's life but will not cure the disease at this time.

BLOOD

Von Willebrand's Disease

VWD has been confirmed in over 50 breeds and is

a manageable disease. It is characterized by moderate to severe bleeding, corrected by blood transfusions from normal dogs and frequently seen with hypothyroidism. When levels are low, a pre-surgical blood transfusion may be necessary. Many breeders screen their breeding stock for vWD.

Immune-Mediated Blood Disease

Immune-mediated diseases affect the red blood cells and platelets. They are called autoimmune hemolytic anemia or immune-mediated anemia when red blood cells are affected, and autoimmune thrombocytopenic purpura, idiopathic thrombocytopenic purpura, and immune-mediated thrombocytopenia when platelets are involved. The disease may appear acutely. Symptoms include jaundice (yellow color) of the gums and eyes and dark brown or dark red urine. Symptoms of platelet disease include pinpoint bruises or hemorrhages in the skin, gums and eye membranes; nosebleeds; bleeding from the GI tract or into the urine. Any of these symptoms constitutes an emergency!

DIGESTIVE SYSTEM AND ORAL CAVITY

Colitis

This disorder has no known cause and appears with some frequency in certain breeds. It is characterized by an intermittent bloody stool, with or without diarrhea.

Chronic Hepatitis

This is the result of liver failure occuring at relatively young ages. In many cases clinical signs are apparent for less than two weeks. They include anorexia, lethargy, vomiting, depression, diarrhea, trembling or shaking, excess thirst and urination, weight loss, and dark bloody stool. Early diagnosis and treatment promise the best chance for survival.

Copper Toxicity

Copper toxicity occurs when excessive copper is concentrated in the liver. In 1995 there was a breakthrough when the DNA marker was identified in one of the afflicted breeds. Therefore carriers will be identified in the future.

ENDOCRINE SYSTEM

Hypothyroidism

Over 50 breeds have been diagnosed with hypothyroidism. It is the number-one endocrine disorder in the dog and is the result of an underactive thyroid gland. Conscientious breeders are screening their dogs if the disease is common to their breed or bloodline. The critical years for the decline of thyroid function are usually between three and eight, although it can appear at an older age. A simple blood test can diagnose or rule out this disorder. It is easily and inexpensively treated by giving thyroid replacement therapy daily. Untreated hypothyroidism can be devastating to your dog.

Addison's Disease

Primary adrenal insufficiency is caused by damage to the adrenal cortex, and secondary adrenocortical insufficiency is the result of insufficient production of the hormone ACTH by the pituitary gland. Symptoms may include depression, anorexia, a weak femoral pulse, vomiting or diarrhea, weakness, dehydration, and occasionally bradycardia.

Cushing's Disease

Hyperadrenocorticism is the over-production of steroid hormone. Dogs on steroid therapy may show Cushing-like symptoms. Some of the symptoms are excess thirst and urination, hair loss, and an enlarged, pendulous, or flaccid abdomen.

EYES

Cataracts

Breeders should screen their breeding stock for this disorder. A cataract is defined as any opacity of the lens or its capsule. It may progress and produce blindness or it may remain small and cause no clinical impairment of vision. Unfortunately some inherited cataracts appear later in life after the dog has already been bred.

Lens Luxation

This condition results when the lens of the eye is not in normal position, and may result in secondary glaucoma.

Glaucoma

Primary glaucoma is caused by increased intraocular pressure due to inadequate aqueous drainage and is not associated with other intraocular diseases. It may initially be in one eye. Secondary glaucoma is caused by increased intraocular pressure brought on by another ocular disease, tumor, or inflammation.

Keratoconjunctivitis Sicca

"Dry eye" (the decrease in production of tears) may be the result of a congenital or inherited deficiency of the aqueous layer, a lack of the proper nervous stimulation of the tearing system, a traumatic incident, or drugs, including topical anesthetics (such as

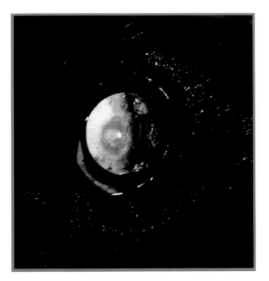

An immature cataract is evident in this dilated pupil. The central white area and cloudy areas at 4:00, 6:00 and 8:00 represent the cataract. Photo courtesy of Dr. Kerry L. Ketring.

atropine, and antibiotics containing sulfadiazine, phenazopyridine or salicyla-sulfapyridine). There seems to be an increased incidence of "dry eye" after "cherry eye" removal.

Progressive Retinal Atrophy (PRA)

This is the progressive loss of vision, first at night, followed by total blindness. It is inherited in many breeds.

Distichiasis

Distichiasis results from extra rows of eyelashes growing out of the meibomian gland ducts. This condition may cause tearing, but tearing may be the result of some other problem that needs to be investigated.

Entropion

Entropion is the inward rolling of the eyelid, usually lower lid, which can cause inflammation and may need surgical correction.

Ectropion

Ectropion is the outward rolling of the eyelid, usually lower lid, and may need surgical correction.

Hypertrophy of the Nictitans Gland

"Cherry eye" is the increase in size of the gland resulting in eversion of the third eyelid and is usually bilateral. Onset frequently occurs during stressful periods such as teething.

NEUROMUSCULAR SYSTEM

Epilepsy

Epilepsy is a disorder in which the electrical brain activity "short circuits," resulting in a seizure. Numerous breeds and mixed breeds are subject to idiopathic epilepsy (no explainable reason). Seizures usually begin between six months and five years of age. Don't panic. Your primary concern should be to keep your dog from hurting himself by falling down the stairs or falling off furniture and/or banging his head. Dogs don't swallow their tongues. If the seizure lasts longer than ten minutes, you should contact your veterinarian. Seizures can be caused by many conditions, such as poisoning and birth injuries, brain infections, trauma or tumors, liver disease, distemper, and low blood sugar or calcium. There are all types of seizures from generalized (the dog will be shaking and paddling/kicking his feet) to standing and staring out in space, etc.

UROGENITAL

Cryptorchidism

This is a condition in which either one or both of the testes fail to descend into the scrotum. There should not be a problem if the dog is neutered early, before two to three years of age. Otherwise, the undescended testicle could turn cancerous.

PET OWNERS & BLOOD PRESSURE

Over the past few years, several scientific studies have documented many health benefits of having pets in our lives. At the State University of New York at Buffalo, for example, Dr. Karen Allen and her colleagues have focused on how physical reactions to psychological stress are influenced by the presence of pets. One such study compared the effect of pets with that of a person's close friend and reported pets to be dramatically better than friends at providing unconditional support. Blood pressure was monitored throughout the study, and, on average, the blood pressure of people under stress who were *with* their pets was 112/75, as compared to 140/95 when they were with the self-selected friends. Heart rate differences were also significantly lower when participants were with their pets. A follow-up study included married couples and looked at the stress-reducing effect of pets versus *spouses*, and found, once again, that pets were dramatically more successful than other people in reducing cardiovascular reactions to stress. An interesting discovery made in this study was that when the spouse and pet were *both* present, heart rate and blood pressure came down dramatically.

Other work by the same researchers has looked at the role of pets in moderating age-related increases in blood pressure. In a study that followed 100 women (half in their 20s and half in their 70s) over six months, it was found that elderly women with few social contacts and *no* pets had blood pressures that were significantly higher (averages of 145/95 compared to 120/80) than elderly women with their beloved pets but few *human* contacts. In other words, elderly women with pets, but no friends, had blood pressures that closely reflected the blood pressures of young women.

This series of studies demonstrates that pets can play an important role in how we handle everyday stress, and shows that biological aging cannot be fully understood without a consideration of the social factors in our lives.

More than best friends or even spouses, pets have a natural calming effect on their humans.

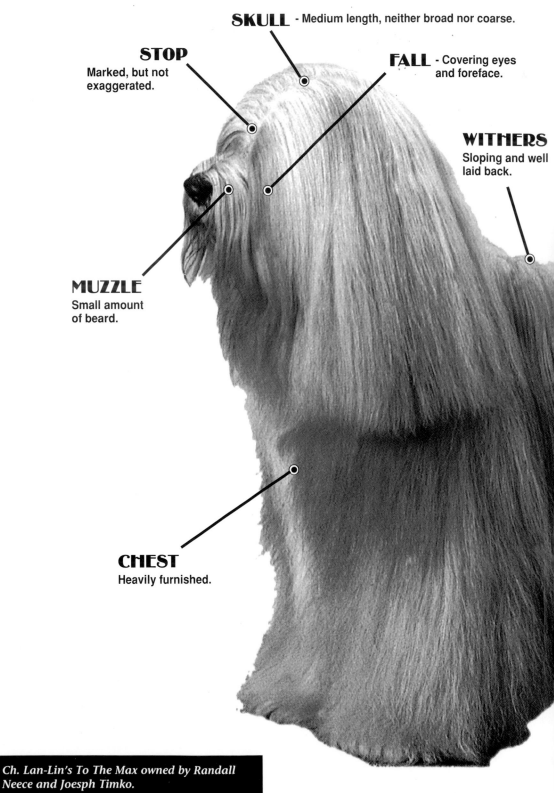

SKULL - Medium length, neither broad nor coarse.

STOP
Marked, but not
exaggerated.

FALL - Covering eyes
and foreface.

WITHERS
Sloping and well
laid back.

MUZZLE
Small amount
of beard.

CHEST
Heavily furnished.

Ch. Lan-Lin's To The Max owned by Randall Neece and Joesph Timko.